Library of Congress Cataloging-in-Publication Data
Becoming a Coach: The Coach U Approach™ / by Thomas J. Leonard:
p. cm.
Includes index
ISBN —1-929668-01-5

Copy editing by Randa McIntosh
Layout and Design by Cosmyk Images, Miami, Florida

Printed in the United States of America
10 9 8 7 6 5 4 3 2 1

Published by Coach U Press
PO Box 881595
Steamboat Springs, Colorado 80488

BECOMING A COACH
THE COACH U APPROACH™

THOMAS J. LEONARD
COACH U PRESS

To my clients,
who are gracious enough
to keep training me
to serve them well.

TABLE OF CONTENTS

8

INTRODUCTION

This is a book about what coaching is, what a coach does and how one becomes a coach. When I sat down to write a book about coaching (finally, after 10 years), I found that I couldn't talk about coaching generically. I felt I had to base the book on how the coaches at Coach U coach their clients. Thus the tagline to this book: The Coach U Approach™.

So, this is a book about coaching – from the Coach U perspective – and the perspective of our 3800+ students and graduates. You see, I asked them to write much of this book. I laid out the framework for the book but it is their comments, quotes and views which tell the real story of what it means to coach and how great coaching is done.

In these pages, you will learn some of the key skills that coaches use effectively with clients. You will also come to understand the powerful dynamic that occurs between coach and client – it is this synergy that makes coaching work. And you will learn some of the proven strategies for how to build a coaching practice, should that be part of your plan.

And, if nothing else, this is a book that will help you understand yourself – and others – better. You will read what motivates and drives people, how people learn and what strategies work to empower people so that they motivate themselves.

And, I believe that you will come away with a deep respect for the quality and sophisticated work that a coach does with a client. Coaching really IS a distinct profession, and I believe these pages will evidence that.

Finally, you will see that this book is both a book about coaching, but also refers to Coach U and our Coach Training Program. Just like every how-to book acts in some way as a brochure for the writer, this book acts as a brochure for Coach U.

I do know that we are unabashed in our approach to both tell you about the coaching process and to describe the benefits of Coach U's Coach Training Program. I hope that I have caused no offense in the manner in which I have done this. This is a solid primer on coaching and a brochure for Coach U as well.

The core values of Coach U are evident throughout the words of each of the contributors to this work. Uncompromising integrity, heart-centeredness, truth/wisdom, generosity and quality course through every page. We hope that you get a feel for not only what we do and how it can contributes to so many lives, but also the high caliber of the students and graduates of Coach U.

You may be asking yourself why we are releasing so much of our intellectual property via the book. After all, what you'll be reading is some of what participants pay thousands of dollars for. What we can say is that this book represents only a small percentage of our intellectual property to which the coaches and graduates of our program have access. In other words, this is only the tip of our knowledge base.

THOMAS J. LEONARD
Seattle, Washington, June 4, 1999

HOW DO I KNOW IF COACHING IS RIGHT FOR ME?

You may have heard the adage that coaches are born, not made, and we tend to agree.

What we've learned from the 3800+ coaches who have joined Coach U or used our coaching programs is that they have always felt like a coach. They were the ones that people turned to for help or support. They were the ones who knew just what to say to help a friend or family member over a rough spot in their professional life. And they were the ones who enjoyed helping others think bigger, think smarter and think differently.

Does any of this sound like you?

To be sure that becoming a coach is a smart move for you, please read the following statements and check the circle next to it if the statement is true for you. (Please note: Some of the statements may appear obvious but they are not.)

- ○ I sense things about others that they are surprised about when I share with them.
- ○ I am intuitive and can sense things about people that others cannot.
- ○ I enjoy helping others solve a problem that they are struggling with.
- ○ I've got that spark. People comment on how alive I am.
- ○ I am a very positive person. I can see daylight at midnight.
- ○ I am naturally curious about people. I want to learn about them.
- ○ I am fascinated about life and how it all works.
- ○ I am excited about the significant changes occuring in all areas of life today and want to stay ahead of the curve.
- ○ I am willing to be honest with people, even if it's awkward for me or for them.
- ○ I deeply respect people and accept very different ways of thinking/living.
- ○ I enjoy being a strategist. I like helping people chart a course.
- ○ I know that I have special abilities and I believe that people are willing to pay for them.
- ○ I am willing to take several years to learn and perfect the craft of coaching.
- ○ I attract people who want my support and input.
- ○ I am open to learning new concepts and paradigms, even if they don't make sense at first.
- ○ I can handle paradoxes.
- ○ I am willing to be a model for my clients.
- ○ I am willing to charge for my time and services.

- ○ I enjoy adding value to whomever I can, because I enjoy providing service.
- ○ I am aware of my limits, yet I know I can coach others well.
- ○ At the beginning, I am willing to coach people for free, to gain experience.
- ○ I am willing to learn coaching via self-study and TeleClass discussions.
- ○ I am willing to learn coaching using the case-study method from a situational perspective.
- ○ I care a lot about other people and enjoy seeing them achieve their goals.
- ○ I am excited about sharing what I've learned with others, and am willing to fashion it into something that fits the clients needs perfectly.

Scoring Key

20-25. You are already a coach, or you should be.

15-19. You are an excellent candidate to become a coach.

10-14. Coaching may not be right for you as a career.

0-9. It appears that coaching would not be the right choice for you.

Summing Up...

How did you do? Most people who read this book score 15 or above. If that's you, I hope that you'll give serious consideration to becoming a coach — or if you are already a coach — to taking your skill set and practice to the next level by becoming a part of Coach U.

> *"I love self-tests and I consider them to be of great help. In taking the self-test for coaching I discovered the skills I already had to be a great coach and also the challenges and areas of development I would face if I decided to enter the field."*
> *– Kathy Pike, kathyp@tesser.com,*
> *http://www.CoachKPike.com*

SECTION 2

WHO BECOMES A COACH?

There are over 1,000 different careers today, and coaches come from virtually all of them. It's common to see consultants, therapists and managers transition into coaching and it's not uncommon for attorneys, accountants and even ministers to enter the field of coaching.

Why is coaching so attractive to individuals with already-successful careers?

Perhaps it is because coaching affords them the opportunity to do what they most want to do with people. After all, coaching as a popular professional service has only been around for about ten years, so most of us didn't know that coaching was an option when we planned our careers.

At Coach U we're also seeing that at least 40% of coaches coming into the field do not plan to establish individual practices or positions, but rather to continue in their current professions. With Coach U training they learn to weave into their work the most fitting pieces of the coaching skill set, models and coaching technology. For example, some therapists will add coaching to their menu of counseling services, whereas other therapists migrate completely to coaching. Another example is the entrepreneur who wants to better manage and motivate his staff and comes into Coach U to learn how to coach others, but also learns how to develop a better business, using our extensive collection of models, strategies and principles.

13

"Coaching is for anyone that loves helping other people, and wants to do something that can make a difference in the quality of that person's life. I'd been searching for a way to combine my desire to help others, use the gifts that God gave me and provide myself with a living and more importantly a lifestyle — coaching and Coach U is giving me that and much, much more!"
– Melinda Vilas, mendycoach@aol.com

"Coaching allows individuals to leverage experiences from their lives and careers and use it to create more meaningful work."
– Alison Hendren, alison@thecoachinggroup.com, www.thecoachinggroup.com

Where are coaches coming from?

Coaching is a viable career option today and the majority of coaches are coming from other professions and career tracks. Some individuals who enter Coach U are coaches without training who want to improve their skills and eventually apply for the Certified Coach designation. Many more individuals enter while still employed in other fields.

Coach U students plan a variety of uses for the skills, connections, and technology they gain through the Coach Training Program. Some are in career transition and will begin building coaching practices even as they study. Others are happy in their careers and will add coaching skills to their repertoire. Many coaches blend careers, working both as coaches and in another field.

Business schools, corporations and prominent national magazines recognize the value of coaching and coaching skills in any organizational or personal environment. Coach U's training and resources add attractive, marketable skills to any resume.

Why are Health Care Professionals learning coaching skills?

Physicians, dentists, chiropractors usually coach part-time or use their coaching skills to help them relate better with their patients.

> *"Healthcare organizations are just beginning to see that training managers in coaching skills will change employee attitudes and result in better service to patients and better business results."*
> *– Allen Nohre, President of Corporate Coach U International, anohre@aol.com*

1. Physicians come to understand what drives human behavior so they can better heal their clients.
2. Dentists learn how to sell/phrase their services to patients and to coach hesitant patients to make a commitment to their dental health.
3. Psychiatrists add a coaching skill set to their own extensive skill set, offering yet another system to help clients heal, progress and develop.
4. Chiropractors use coaching skills to help clients/patients more completely integrate the well-being work they are receiving.
5. Nurses have been coaching patients for years and as a professional coach, they are well compensated for their abilities.

> *"After 20 years as a nurse all the changes in healthcare have left me feeling empty. Through coaching I discovered what it was about nursing that fulfilled me — truly reaching another person, one-on-one. Coaching gives me this — and so much more!"*
> *– Kim Johnson, kimkj6@earthlink.net, www.nursewatch.com*

6. Medical technicians often become coaches as a sideline, in order to help people in a non-medical way and earn additional income.
7. Naturopaths become coaches because they want to treat the entire person, not just the physical symptoms.
8. Massage therapists add coaching services to their menu of well-being services and cross-sell to current clients.

> *"As a massage therapist I work with clients to relieve chronic pain and stress. I have extensive knowledge of the physical, emotional and energetic aspects of the human system. I blend this knowledge with the commu-*

nication skills that I have learned at Coach U to work at a deep transformational level with both my massage clients and coaching clients. In both situations I provide the space for individuals to learn more about who they are and the tools to move forward."
– Kathy Pike, kathyp@tesser.com, www.CoachKPike.com

9. Personal trainers are already coaches — for fitness — and many add the personal/business skill set because of how effectively they can help clients to integrate all aspects of their lives.
10. Nutritionists already know what makes a body healthy and by becoming a coach they can more effectively craft a comprehensive, integrated wellness plan.

Why are Professional Services Providers becoming coaches?
    These professionals are attorneys, accountants, realtors, brokers, insurance agents and professional organizers, among others. About half of this group migrate from their current profession to becoming a full-time coach within 4 years. The other half continue in their profession, but say they've benefited from coach training in the following ways:
1. They are able to help their clients more effectively with less stress.

"As an attorney, I loved my clients. They came to me with problems ranging from being hurt in car accidents, to being sexually harassed, to striving to gain or retain custody of their children. They were usually pretty upset and feeling victimized. As a trial attorney I was successful in transforming them into clear, effective advocates for their causes. Now I bring those skills I developed as an attorney to coaching. It's perfect because I still get the reward of helping clients to be effective in their lives without all the attendant complications of a legal case."
– Katy Eymann, kteymann@aol.com

2. They strengthen their Personal Foundation so that they are more productive.

"I approached Norma about coaching me through my career transition from high tech into the legal field. I have accomplished more in this direction in the past few months with coaching than I did in years."
– Carol B., lawyer, Seattle, WA (Client of Coach Norma Reiss, norma@wisdomcoaching.com, www.wisdomcoaching.com)

3. They escape burnout and enjoy "winning" every day.

"As a lawyer, I often felt that if I won a case, it was like

*getting to zero because the result is what should have
happened. It was only fair that we won. All I had done
was fix a situation that had been broken. On the other
hand, if I lost a case, it was a failure ranging from, 'I did
something wrong,' to 'I should not have taken the case
to begin with.' Consequently, there was little sense of
satisfaction in practicing law except monetarily.
Coaching, in contrast, provides a huge sense of
satisfaction because it's all new gains and the monetary
reward is good, too."*
– Katy Eymann, kteymann@aol.com

4. They are more effective at selling because they have strengthened their
   communicating and relating skills through Coach U training.

   *"As a real estate speaker and trainer, I felt coaching skills
   would increase the value to my audiences. The best
   salespeople are coaches, after all, and by modeling the
   coaching skills, real estate people can discover what
   their clients really want and coach them in the best way
   to achieve it. My coaching skills have not only enhanced
   my presentations but also given me some concrete
   techniques that work in selling. The shift has changed
   from manipulation to attraction!"*
   *– Joeann Fossland, joeann@joeann.com,
   www.joeann.com*

5. They learn and apply the Attraction Approach to marketing their
   professional services, resulting in measurably higher incomes, with less
   promotion.
6. They have doubled or tripled their referral networks to include coaches
   and other professionals in their local area as well as nationally.
7. They have expanded their web presence and Internet marketing skills,
   which leads to numerous referrals.
8. They are coming to understand who people are, how they operate and
   how to get them to listen to professional advice.
9. They are adding new revenue streams by offering coaching as a professional sideline, distinct from their old professional services menu.

   *"I was a financial planner for 25 years and increasingly
   unhappy with government regulation and unfulfilled by
   the service delivered. Coaching has allowed me to use
   my unique abilities in a way that is full of integrity. The
   response from my existing clients has been overwhelm-
   ing. I outsourced the financial planning to a colleague
   that I trust and have trebled my revenues in my first six
   months in business coaching."*
   – Christopher Barrow, mbfa@compuserve.com

10. They provide more client value by including coaching and training as part of the service package they offer to clients.

> *"As a management consultant my job was to impart my knowledge and vision on to others. Unfortunately they seldom shared my vision. As a coach I now help clients formulate and achieve their own vision. For me this is far more rewarding. For my clients, it's far more effective."*
> *– Keith Collins, Keith@incondition.freeserve.com.uk, www.coachreferral.com/coaches/c/collins1001910.html*

> *"I practiced law for 11 years. It taught me how to win and lose, but not how to create and grow. It taught me how to direct my clients, but not how to allow them to build something that truly belonged to them. I can easily say that, in the four years I have been a full time coach, I have done more to assist my clients to find the answers they truly need and can use than I ever did in the practice of law. Moreover, I have reveled in every coaching minute and the grace it has provided."*
> *– Margaret Krigbaum, makcoach@rtd.com*

11. They are becoming coaches (vs. just experts) in their professional specialties and working with current clients differently.

> *"I made the decision to become a coach shortly after I left the corporate world to work as a Marketing Consultant. The additional space I had after taking a short step away from the corporate world and the confidence of successfully working for myself combined to help me see my vision of the ideal career. I wanted unlimited earning potential, geographic freedom, a job that meshed with my values and a way to be involved in personal growth every day. Coaching is the perfect career for me. Most of all, it's exciting and fun."*
> *– Doug Hudiburg, dhudiburg@msn.com*

12. They develop a national reputation by using the power of the Internet.

How does coach training strengthen Business and Personal Consultants?

Consultants include those working in the areas of management, small business and executive consulting, organizational development specialists, industrial psychologists, change agents, marketing consultants and others. Professionals from these fields are moving into the coaching field for many reasons:

1. They enjoy longer-term contracts, with less selling.
2. Coaches have more permission to impact the organization or client at all levels.

*"As a Professional Organizer Coach, I am able to help
my clients in a far deeper way than I would giving
hands-on organizing assistance only. With coaching,
my clients are able to get to the root of the issues that
cause the disorganization in their lives. I have helped
them make permanent changes in and bring harmony
and balance to their actions, relationships and thinking
as well as to their environment."*
– Mary Sigmann, HarmonyPro@aol.com

3. They can offer their clients a broader menu of services and products.

    *"Consulting is a crowded field, lots of competition, you
    need special skills to increase your attractiveness.
    Coaching fits well here. I am a better consultant for my
    coach training. I have noticed that I get more process
    oriented consulting work (where I can really use my
    coaching skills). Also I get consulting assignments
    from clients and clients from seminars."*
    – Soren Holm, soren@utveckling.nu

4. They enjoy a consistent revenue stream with less turnover.
5. They employ faster acting technology with longer-term benefits.

    "Coaching clients to greater success through effective
    strategies, designed and implemented together, can pro-
    duce extraordinary marketing results, because it's more
    about choosing cultural improvement and doing things
    better."
    – David Hutchins, pressmatters@msn.com.au

6. They undergo less travel, less strain, less disruption and they are free
   from deadlines.
7. They earn a high hourly rate with virtually no expenses.
8. They experience increased referrals due to more affordable price points
   for clients.
9. The relationship with the client is more rewarding due to the collaborative, interdevelopmental nature of the work.

    *"I'd been servicing Fortune 100 companies for 13 years
    prior to enrolling in Coach U and becoming a full-time,
    professional coach. The demand for consulting servic-
    es was tremendous and still is, and the field was
    extremely lucrative. However, time after time, our
    clients failed to fully implement our recommendations.
    Often, it was because the action plan came from out-
    side the firm. Even when the clients found our recom-
    mendations to be wise, even brilliant, they were other
    people's answers. When I switched approaches from*

consultant to coach, it made a world of difference to my clients. When coached, clients create or co-create with the coach their own solutions. They take more ownership for solutions. They feel empowered by the process. They are willing to take more risk to find the best solution possible. Both the client and the coach share in the win. It is altogether a more satisfying experience."
– Meryl Moritz, urbancowgirl@worldnet.att.net

10. They find their work invigorating and stimulating due to the dynamic nature of coaching.

> *"I am a Marketing Executive for a high-tech company that targets the financial industry. I became a coach because it was my dream and I wanted to help people live theirs. What I am finding is that not only do my clients want to find satisfying and fulfilling careers, but they also want to learn to market their skills internally or market their new businesses to the world. Coaching allows me to support them through their new endeavors and I have the pleasure of watching their dreams become reality."*
> *– Deborah J. Brown, info@surpassyourdreams.com, www.surpassyourdreams.com*

Why do corporate employees learn coaching skills?

A corporate employee might be a manager, executive or CEO. Perhaps they work in human relations, as an executive director, a project manager or a sales professional. Corporate employees such as these become coaches for many different reasons, which include:

1. A manager wants to be more effective with staff and learns/uses coaching skills that work in the corporate setting.

> *"As a medical group practice manager, I work with physicians, nurses and technicians. Leading a team of healthcare professionals is often like 'herding cats.' Since I started taking classes through Coach U I have learned skills that allow me to bring out the strengths of the team. Additionally, I can give each one of them the individual attention they desire."*
> *– Leona Mathews, Leonacoach@aol.com*

2. An executive wants to extend his/her ability to sense and see trends and opportunities that lie beyond the reported data.
3. Executive directors of not-for-profits and government agencies use coaching skills and the coaching approach to transform their organizational culture into a more responsive, entrepreneurial and innovative one.
4. Companies hire outside coaches for key employees or hire in-house

coaches to serve employees in areas of productivity enhancement, performance, personal blocks, personality conflicts and leadership development.

> *"My background is in Psychology, followed by a career in sales and marketing to director level in major UK companies. Coaching gave me a great opportunity to focus these two sets of experiences and skills together to empower others (my clients) to succeed. This means that I quickly empathize with career pressures and aspirations while having the expertise to stimulate individuals to break through their own 'glass ceilings.'"*
> *– Mike Duckett, Coaching.for.Success@usa.net*

5. Project managers learn coaching skills in order to work with the implementers to get the project completed with less stress, less pushing and fewer delays.

> *"For many years I managed software development projects as a consultant. Three or four years ago I really started to hate it. I kept thinking, 'I can't do this for the rest of my life.' When I discovered coaching it was like a breath of fresh air. Now I have set up my work such that I manage projects on a part time basis and have a part time coaching practice as well. The interesting thing is, now I LOVE managing projects. Once I removed the pressure of 'having' to do it and do it all the time, the joy quickly returned. And, by bringing my coaching skills to my projects, my ability to manage diverse people and resources has greatly expanded."*
> *– David Buck, dave@davebuck.com, http://www.dave-buck.com*

6. Sales professionals use coaching skills to better serve customers and increase referrals.

> *"Having been in sales for most of my life, the concept of attracting clients instead of selling them was mind-boggling and then enlightening. Its application has been both effortless and lucrative. What a great way to do business!"*
> *– Sandra Dell, dellcoach@aol.com*

7. HR executives take the coach training in order to learn how to weave the coaching principles and process into the fabric of their organizations.
8. The retiring CEO becomes a coach in order to have a rewarding and professional focus for the next stage of her/his life.
9. Employees wanting to redesign their life, time and priorities, enter coach training in order to develop the necessary skills and wisdom to earn a living outside of the corporate setting.

> *"I have always been a person who influenced others in innovative and positive ways. I have always been an agent for change. What I didn't realize until now is that I have always been a coach."*
> *– Lyn Christian, coachlyn@hotmail.com*

10. Corporate employees wanting to be more effective at managing their actions, their accounts and their results enter Coach U in order to become more productive in their current jobs and lives.

> *"The corporate arena is changing quickly. The technology of coaching helps to reduce stress, increase effectiveness, strengthen decision-making, enhance leadership skills and improve personal and team performance. All are vital in this fast-paced global marketplace."*
> *– Linda Miller, Linda@InterLinkTC.com,*
> *www.InterLinkTC.com*

Another way for managers and employees to get trained as a coach is through Corporate Coach U International. Go to http://www.ccui.com.

Why do independent and creative types enter Coach U?

It may be surprising to learn that many Coach U students are creative types and other independent people such as entrepreneurs, small business owners, actors, dancers, singers, writers, engineers, geniuses, scientists, researchers and architects. These people come to Coach U for many reasons:

1. Entrepreneurs become coaches because they like the business structure and opportunity of being a coach and/or because they enjoy helping others succeed by being their coach.

> *"If I had had a coach at the conception of our business, I would still be president of a creative multi-million dollar enterprise! After completing Coach U TeleClasses, I fully understand where the mistakes were made and how drastically different a business can be with great coaching. I can now offer services to start-up companies who want to be successful on all levels right from the start!"*
> *– Sharon Hooper, wolfie@interisland.net*

2. The small business owner becomes a coach in order to learn more about managing people, marketing their business and understanding what motivates people in general and buyers in particular.

> *"I operated a small and successful business for 15 years and learned myriad lessons. As a coach I still operate a (very) small business and consider myself lucky to be able to help others with their 'lessons.' I'm*

more successful than ever, because success now
encompasses my life as well as my business."
– Sandra Dell, dellcoach@aol.com

3. Actors and dancers become coaches when they are ready for the next phase of their lives.

> *"As a performing artist, becoming a coach was a natu-*
> *ral next step for me. I experience coaching as another*
> *form of artful expression, as the 'dance' that occurs*
> *with the client is incredibly inspiring and creative."*
> *– Pamela Richarde, peacecoach@innerspirit.com,*
> *www.innerspirit.com*

4. Singers find that they discover coaching provides a steady income stream and permits them the flexibility to sing when they wish.
5. Writers become coaches for two reasons. First, because they are already facile with language, they enjoy conveying principles and observations to clients. Second, by having clients, they find that their writing is more inspired because they are working at a real-life level with people.

> *"When I read about Coach U and how coaches help*
> *people reach their goals, I thought about my writing*
> *friends who had been coming to me informally for*
> *advice. I always used my instincts and experience in*
> *writing and publishing to help them as best I could. I*
> *enrolled in Coach U to have more to offer them and to*
> *use what I learned to further my own creative goals.*
> *My mentor coach helped me realize more of my cre-*
> *ative vision and refine, refine, refine what I am all about*
> *and what I want."*
> *– MJ Abell, mjabell@lucent.com*

6. Creative geniuses and other geniuses become coaches because they like to use their minds to solve problems or to create something new.
7. Scientists become coaches because they enjoy the technical nature of the coaching process.
8. Researchers become coaches because they enjoy dealing in information and like the process of finding – and providing – what their clients want, information-wise.

> *"A common theme in my life has been to perceive the*
> *essential and communicate the useful and so I find that I*
> *use the same skills when coaching clients as I do when*
> *doing educational research. I tend to identify the signifi-*
> *cant components of a client's situation and then com-*
> *municate to them what I feel they need to know to be*
> *able to do what they want to do. I have always been*
> *sensitive to what needs to be done, so I have valuable*

coaching skills already. What I get from Coach U is learning how to really connect and relate with people on a deep level; how to build relationships, which is something that has not been easy for me. I greatly value this skill and I believe it is not enough to just solve problems or give advice without knowing who the client is."
– Stephen J. Addison, coach@btinternet.com

9. Engineers become coaches because it brings out their emotional and spiritual side – they learn to solve problems in non-linear ways.
10. Architects enjoy coaching because they get to help clients design the perfect environment for their entire lives, beyond the building they live or work in.

> *"As an architect and city planner I have been instrumental in shaping the external environment of people. As a coach I am a catalyst for changes that alter the interior environment of my clients. Both require me to be highly creative. Listening and discerning are key skills in both architecture and coaching."*
> *– Prataap Patrose, prataap@aol.com*

Why do helping professionals integrate coaching skills?
The helping professions include counseling, therapy, psychology, ministry and others. Therapists-turned-coaches really like their new profession. After a one-year accelerated training and transition period, many therapists and counselors enjoy:

1. Healthier clients who are motivated to grow and achieve.

> *"My personal mission is to teach people to have joyful lives. As a clinical psychologist, I helped many people relieve or eliminate 'symptoms' and 'problems.' But they weren't exactly joyful. Now, as a coach, I collaborate with people to reach their personal and business/career dreams, to realize their heart's desires, by doing what they love and by using their strengths, talents and gifts. And guess what? They become joyful!"*
> *– Judith E. Craig, Ph.D., judi@drcraig.com, www.drcraig.com*

2. Easier work with less resistance because the client CAN change.

> *"As an Occupational Therapist, I assisted people with disabilities to gain more independence in their daily lives. As a coach, I shift from the focus on disabilities to ABILITIES. People not only gain more independence, but also the ability to soar high above what is limiting to them."*
> *– Jane Yousey, ReachnHigh@aol.com*

3.   More enjoyable process, focusing on development more than healing.

> *"When I went back to school to work on a Master's in Educational Psychology, my goal was to become a researcher. By the time I had done research and finished my thesis I realized research moved too slowly for me. I wanted to have more contact with people and see results more quickly, yet still be on the cutting edge of work involving personal development and learning. Though my background in psychology led many to think I should become a therapist, I didn't want to delve into peoples' pasts. I'm so happy that I found coaching. Working with my clients to excel in all areas of their lives gives me the energy and satisfaction that research was too slow to deliver."*
> *– Gail Valenti, lgvalenti@aol.com*

4.   Less responsibility, less burden, less weight because the client is empowered and self-responsible.

> *"I had a very busy psychotherapy practice for 23 years and was looking for a new paradigm that would be less parental and more collegial, especially for those clients who had already completed their childhood work. When I discovered Coach U on the internet and read the 36 modules of course content, I knew this was the model that I had been looking for. I no longer carry a pager for emergencies, nor have to arrange coverage when I am away on a trip. I feel freer to be myself and express myself more spontaneously in the coaching relationship."*
> *– Jacquie Damgaard, Ph.D., jacquie@coaching-solutions.com, www.coaching-solutions.com*

5.   No managed care intrusion or restrictions; you are free to coach as you and the client wish.
6.   Higher fees, on average, ($75-$125/hr for therapists, $75-$300/hr for coaches).
7.   The chance to expand what you know already about people and behavior.
8.   The convenience and flexibility of doing your work by phone and e-mail, if desired.

> *"Because the coaching is done primarily on the phone, I am able to travel as much as I like, or even move, and I can take my business with me! It is so satisfying to see my clients move from an already successful life to one of extraordinary pleasure and fulfillment."*
> *– Jacquie Damgaard, Ph.D., jacquie@coaching-solutions.com, www.coaching-solutions.com*

9. Freedom from the burdens of paperwork, politics and insurance.

> *"As a school counselor and administrator, I was known for my innovative, people-centered approach. I had developed a knack for getting people to shift their thinking, to step outside their boxes and to see what's possible for their lives. Sometimes in the school setting, the people side of things became eclipsed with paper work and administrivia. As a coach I get to use my people development skills exclusively and can choose to say 'no' to what is not my brilliance."*
> *– Joanne Ivancich, coach4you@aol.com, www.LifeDesignInstitute.com*

10. Ability to have a national or international practice.

Why do trainers, presenters, speakers and educators seek coaching skills training?

Those who are training and motivating others in groups can benefit from adding coaching to their skill set because with the skills and tools they pick up at Coach U, they can:

1. Offer post-seminar services, such as weekly coaching.
2. Train groups better because they are working directly with individual clients.
3. Enjoy a stable and consistent income stream from coaching clients.
4. Increase their network of referrals for their speaking business.
5. Offer a package of services to clients at a higher price point.
6. Link up with other coaches to share client load, speaking engagements.
7. Have more case studies should they decide to write a book.
8. Be more appealing to a meeting planner because of the coaching skill set.
9. Offer an attractive alternative to seminars for companies with limited budgets.

> *"Using [coaching] instead of sending executives and managers to seminars two or three times a year can be more beneficial to ongoing career development, not to mention less expensive..." - PC Week*

10. Incorporate coaching skills into their speaking to impact audiences profoundly.

> *"My coaching practice, the hands on experience with my clients and the TeleClasses that I lead have given me a wealth of knowledge that has proven invaluable as I speak to groups on a wide variety of subjects. In fact the coaching has actually helped evolve me and create a speaking practice that will take me and my*

business to the next level."
– Marlene Elliott, marlene@marlene.net

What personal backgrounds do coaches come from?

In addition to the aforementioned career tracks, coaches also come from various backgrounds, specialized skill sets or with special life experiences, such as:

The Situationally Challenged
People Diagnosed with Attention Deficit Disorder (ADD)
People In Recovery from Addictions
Super Sensitive People (SSP)
"After joining Coach U I was surprised and overjoyed to learn that there was a Special Interest Group for SSP people like myself. And I was equally surprised to discover so many people drawn to coaching were also SSP people. The sense of community and support has been very heartwarming and helpful."
– Michael Sheffield, mscoach@sonic.net

Single Parents
"Flexibility is an essential element in being a parent, especially a single parent. As a coach I am able to create a work schedule that allows me to attend school activities and extra-curricular events. Coaching has also made me more flexible personally and my daughter thinks that's great."
– Sandra Dell, dellcoach@aol.com

Those With Diverse Interests
"Writing, silversmithing and lapidary are my passions – so too is personal growth. Yet personal growth writers and artists often have a difficult time of fitting their passions into a supportive lifestyle – or so it was for me. Coach U taught me how to combine my passions, while giving me the skills necessary to make it all work. I had to open my mind and let go of my picture of how it all must be. I also cleaned up my life – simplified it- to make room for life itself. My greatest passion now is passing it all on through my coaching."
– Edmond E Frank, ShiftCoach@bigfoot.com,
www.ShiftCoach.com

The Unconventional
"My interests were always so eclectic, I thought I might never fit in anywhere. Coaching has given me a place to be myself and use all the things I'm interested in to help my clients: from golf to the Beatles, from Shakespeare to Seinfeld to Senge."

*– Jay Perry, Jay@CoachingCollective.com,
www.CoachingCollective.com*

The Personal Growth-Oriented
*"In spite of having been actively involved in personal
growth activities for many years, I was frustrated with my
inability to integrate my beliefs into how I actually lived
my life. Coach U provided what was missing for that to
happen – the guidance, structure, accountability and
ongoing support of a community that lives its teachings.
My life flows more easily and peacefully because my
beliefs and actions and lifestyle are congruent."
– Judy Godinez, judyg110@aol.com*

The Spiritually-Centered
*"Coach U allows me to fully and successfully operate in
the material, commercial world, while still honoring and
developing my own personal spirituality and that of my
clients."
– Keith Collins, Keith@incondition.freeserve.com.uk,
www.coachreferral.com/coaches/c/collins1001910.html*

People Who Enjoy Transformation
*"Coach U is essential for anyone who is in transition or
wants to transform their life in any way. Inspiration is
an hourly occurrence, whether you attend TeleClasses
or get involved with your own coach. I can hear transformation actually taking place as I listen to participants
in TeleClasses and other related calls. The excitement,
as the 'ahas' are heard, is felt by all. The environment
itself is transformational!"
– Sharon Hooper, wolfie@interisland.net*

The Highly Motivated
*"I have always been a highly motivated person. As a
highly motivated life success coach, I have learned to
pull clients forward instead of pushing them from
behind. They appreciate this and seem to attain what
they want more quickly and with less struggle."
– Dawn M. Osborn, M.S., Dawn@keys-to-
success.com, www.keys-to-success.com*

Early Adopters
*"In my previous life as a small business owner people
were always saying that I was at least five years ahead
of the pack. When I started with Coach U, I knew I
was at least five years ahead of a growing trend and
was delighted to find hundreds of other coaches who
shared my vision of the future."
– Cynthia Bahnuik, cbahnuik@incentre.net*

The Highly Creative
"Creative people often appreciate brainstorming partners and sounding boards. They also like having a safe space to explore ideas and to get support when it seems in short supply elsewhere. The environment, colleagues, classes and coaches I found at Coach U helped extend my thinking and open up new possibilities. My coach has also helped me set up some filters to help identify the most promising possibilities."
– Ted Isensee, ted_isensee@TheBusinessCoach.com, www.TheBusinessCoach.com

High Performer/Superstar
"Many high achievers are isolated and alone in their pursuit of excellence. Having a coach is like having a behind-the-scenes partner. A partner who listens intently. A partner who cares deeply enough to be direct and honest. A partner who speaks the unspeakable and asks the unaskable. With a coach, the super-star runs the race to win."
– Linda Miller, Linda@InterLinkTC.com, www.InterLinkTC.com

"I have been a high performing individual contributor and team member in my former career. As a coach I've learned to let go of the need to always have per-fection. I have much more energy now to focus on achieving my goals. What's surprised me most is that I achieve even more now that I don't push myself so hard."
– Natalie Gahrmann, nataliegahrmann@hotmail.com

Athlete
"A major part of my life has been spent developing my physical abilities in many outdoor athletic arenas (mountaineering, rock climbing, river running and extreme skiing). It was the most effective way I found to tap in to my personal power. After becoming a coach I use many metaphors and references to my outdoor adventures to provide inspiration and transfor-mation for my clients. The lessons of two different paths can run parallel."
– Kathy Pike, kathyp@tesser.com, www.CoachKPike.com

Sports Coach
"As a part time soccer coach at a major university, I am very aware of what a challenge it is to coach well. We work every day in practice to create an environment

where the game can come to life. This is when it is a joy to be there...a joy to just play and use the game as a way to learn about yourself. Coaching on a personal level is very much the same. It's all about bringing life to life. The game is to make each project, each challenge an opportunity to grow and learn about yourself."
– David Buck, dave@davebuck.com,
www.davebuck.com

Genius/Inventive
"As a highly motivated person, I had a dozen projects in the works at one time...all interesting but going nowhere because I lacked the focus and attention that each project deserved. My coach helped me sequence successful steps for each project and as a result I am producing twice as much as I had ever dreamed I could, including a publishing project, an invention and a dynamic, growing practice."
– Jane Yousey, ReachnHigh@aol.com

What demographic groups do coaches come from?
Baby Boomer
"I believe that as baby boomers reach a certain age our focus is shifting to our contribution: our place emotionally and spiritually in the world. We have achieved the material wealth, climbed the corporate ladder, had successful businesses, bought the house with the picket fence – we've done it all. Now we are asking some new questions: is this all there is – what do I do now - how to I make a more meaningful personal contribution? Coach training offers the opportunity to investigate these questions."
– Cynthia Bahnuik, cbahnuik@incentre.net

Gen Xer
"I am under 30 years old and have been struggling with finding a satisfying career since graduating from college. Coaching has been the perfect synthesis of all my 'ideal career elements.' I am thrilled to be a part of the coaching community and now coach people who are feeling lost and frustrated about their career path, like I once was, to find their perfect work."
– Lucinda Kerschensteiner, lucindak@prodigy.net

Retired
"I am 60 years old and retiring from my landscape design business. Being a very active and vital person, I needed something that was stimulating, completely engaging and creative yet would allow me to work at

home. Becoming a coach was the perfect shift for me and Coach U made the shift very easy. I intend to coach for many years to come. Who knows into what wonderful areas this new profession will lead me?"
– Michael Sheffield, mscoach@sonic.net

What educational background should a coach have?

We are often asked this question by aspiring coaches. The answers are as varied as the coaches themselves. We know that 90% of coaches have at least a bachelor's degree and that over half (55%) have an advanced degree. Obviously, a strong educational background is a major advantage, both in terms of what you've learned and because holding degrees opens career and business doors for many.

That said, however, it is the coach's life experience and willingness to learn the craft of coaching that are the best predictors of their ability to be a successful coach. Knowledge is terrific, but your willingness to learn new things, such as coaching skills, distinctions, coaching models and coaching concepts, is even more important than what you already know.

Here is a list of the most common degrees and designations of coaches at Coach U: BA | BS | CFA | CFP | CMC | CPA | DO | JD | MA | MBA | MD | MSW | ND | OD | PhD

We feel that it says a lot about these individuals holding these degrees and designations that they are willing to devote two more years to master the coaching skill set via Coach U and then to earn the Certified Coach designation. The training to become a coach is unique, comprehensive and a worthwhile investment if you are serious about coaching well.

"I retired from a very busy psychotherapy practice of 23 years to write the books that I had been wanting to create but finding little time to really do. As the writing progressed, I began to miss the experience of being with other people in an intimate and helpful way. When I found Coach U on the internet, I came instantly out of 'retirement' and added a coaching practice to my life of writing. The sense of the client as a totally self-responsible person enables me to be fully present during the coaching sessions and then fully present to my personal life during other hours."
– Jacquie Damgaard, Ph.D., jacquie@coaching-solutions.com, www.coaching-solutions.com

Summing Up...

Did you see yourself anywhere in this section? We wanted the coaches themselves to tell you who they are and why they became coaches. They have come from diverse educational, demographic, personal and career backgrounds to join the community of Coach U and become skilled coaches. Feel free to contact these coaches to learn more about them, their services and their career path.

WHAT ARE THE BENEFITS OF
BECOMING A COACH?

1. Coaching is a rewarding and fulfilling career choice.

Coaches LOVE what they do because they enjoy helping people get what they most want in life. Just think about it – you get to work with positive people like yourself who are eager to learn and excited about achieving. They want your support and advice and are willing to pay for it.

> *"The greatest benefit to me of being a coach is that coaching gathers together all of my skills, values, talents and past experiences and wraps them into a package that is fun, challenging, helpful to others and pays well, too."*
> *– Jo Ann Heiser, lifecoachjo@juno.com*

> *"One couple I actually started coaching on their second date, they have since gotten married and we continue our dialogue weekly. That ability to play a role with a couple as they lay a foundation for their relationship and a life together - words can't describe the feeling!"*
> *– Ed Shea, CoachIMAGO@aol.com*

2. Coaches enjoy the freedom to live and work anywhere they wish.

Some coaches think of themselves on a permanent vacation because they can coach from the beach, the pool, from a ski lodge, from their RV – or from the comfort of their favorite chair in their favorite room in their home. (We've heard reports of coaches coaching from their hot tubs, but this has not been substantiated.)

> *"I live on an island outside Stockholm, Sweden. In spring and summer I coach from my garden, while the deer graze at the other end."*
> *– Soren Holm, soren@utveckling.nu*

> *"The freedom I have as a coach is truly remarkable. I can coach from my home-office during a snowstorm or poolside while on vacation (both of which I have done). Such freedom is rare and my appreciation of this leads me to be the best coach I know how to be."*
> *– Dawn M. Osborn, M.S., Dawn@keys-to-success.com, www.keys-to-success.com*

3. Being a coach accelerates your personal and professional development.

If you are someone who enjoys the process of developing yourself and knows the long-term value of such, then you'll enjoy being a coach because you are in an environment that causes you to grow, without you having to push yourself. Because your clients are on a fast track, your pace is naturally accelerated. They learn from you and you learn from them. It's that simple.

> *"I know in speaking with other coaches that it is no accident that whatever I am challenged by, I have clients challenged by the same things. It forces me to evolve quickly so I can model the change for my clients. My development is accelerated out of my commitment to provide the very best coaching for my clients."*
> *– Katy Eymann, kteymann@aol.com*

4. A coaching business has the potential to quickly bring in a high income.

Those coaches who decide to have a coaching practice average $125 an hour in coaching fees, with the range being between $75 and $300 per hour. One of the nice things about coaching is that because it is so effective, clients can achieve significant results in as little as 30 minutes a week with you. So, if you charge them $250 a month (the national average for newer coaches), you'll be spending two hours with them a month, for an average of $125 an hour. It's a low price point for the client, but a reasonably high fee for the coach.

> *"Enrolling in Coach U in 1995 made possible the perfect career and lifestyle for me. I work at home four days a week, finishing by 3 p.m. when my children get home from school. I walk outside to greet them getting off the bus, fulfilled by my rewarding work with fascinating clients. I earn more than I ever have in any previous job, corporate or entrepreneurial."*
> *– Barbara Hannah, barbara@lovinglife.net*

5. You will flourish in an expanded professional network and community.

Success today is largely dependent on the size and strength of your personal and professional network. Some even say that you are worth your number of people in your network, squared (Network X Network). Whatever the measures of value are, the more people you get to know – and who get to know you – the better for your long term financial success and professional development. As a coach you instantly expand your network by a factor of 10, given the cooperative and collaborative way coaches interact.

> *"I decided to join Coach U because my goal was to compress decades of education into a short period of time. I feel nothing on earth is more valuable to an individual's success than the life experience of a group of people already producing the results I am seeking. And I got that at Coach U."*
> *– David Shockley, David@Nextstepcoaching.com, http://www.Nextstepcoaching.com*

6. New coaches enter the profession easily, at their own pace.

You do not need to take 3 years off and go back to school in order to become a coach. You can stay in your current profession or job and learn at your own pace. You can complete the training in as little as 1 year or take as long as you want – it's entirely up to you and your schedule. You can go part-time or full-time. Specialize or be a generalist. Coach individuals or businesses. The options are all yours.

"I am working full time and am coaching too. The flexibility of the Coach U courses fits easily into my lifestyle. I tend to take a bundle of classes one evening early in the week when I don't have too many commitments. This month I am taking two classes but next month I am taking four. In the summer I may well have a month off to go abroad. At Coach U that's fine. You book your classes on the world-wide web and there are classes to suit anyone's schedule."
– Gavin Ingham, gavin@harvest.freeserve.co.uk

7. You can truly earn while you learn.

Most coaches start coaching clients within the first 90 days of entering Coach U and many are earning fees shortly thereafter. We feel it's very important to coach while you learn and learn while you coach. And, while you're at it, why not enjoy the financial rewards that come when you add tremendous value to others? Very few professions offer this earn-while-you-learn opportunity. Coaching does.

"Within a month of joining Coach U, I had 5 paying clients. Those early clients only paid me $30 a month, but now I charge ten times that, because my clients grow so quickly. The funny thing is, I haven't even graduated yet!"
Michele Lisenbury, michele@lisenbury.com, www.lisenbury.com

8. Coaching is a way to make the kind of difference you most want to make.

Coaches like the process of helping others improve the quality of their lives and achieve goals they might not have reached on their own. Many coaches are the kind of people who have always wanted to do work that makes a difference in this world... on either a local or a global basis. Being a coach allows them to truly feel the impact of their work on a daily basis.

"Coaching allows me to share my gifts with the world, through many venues. These gifts include helping people to get what they really, really want, to help people overcome personal and professional obstacles and to simply increase their quality of life without sacrificing. It's gratifying to see people all around me claiming their

power each and every day."
– Jennifer Corbin, jennifer@compasscoaching.com,
www.compasscoaching.com

*"I reached a point in my life that I demanded from
myself to live life at the highest and the deepest levels.
I wanted more juice in my life, not once in a while, but
every single day. Coaching allows me to make a difference in other people's lives while taking mine to the
next level. Coaching is not an option...it is a must!"*
– David Shockley, David@Nextstepcoaching.com,
www.Nextstepcoaching.com

9. Their chosen profession brings coaches great joy.

When you feel even better at the end of a day of coaching others than
you did at the start of the day, then joy is likely present. Coaching is invigorating to both parties – it CREATES energy thanks to synergy; it doesn't
drain energy. And as the relationship between you and your client unfolds, it
becomes richer and even more fulfilling: Joy.

*"Being a coach has brought an amazing amount of joy
into my life. Not only do I get a thrill being a partner to
my clients as they move forward and discover more joy
in their own lives, but I bask in their praise for what my
coaching has done for them. Also, the concepts
involved in coaching and used in my own life have
brought me joy. I no longer race through life on adrenaline constantly finding things to criticize. I now live at
a leisurely pace, no longer judging people and my sur-
roundings and am surprised at the joy I never realized
existed."*
– Gail Valenti, lgvalenti@aol.com

*"With the strange mixture of skills I have, I never
thought I'd find a career that made use of even a few,
much less most or all of them. Coaching and facilitating
TeleClasses uses everything I have and more. This
career constantly challenges me to push the envelope
and to expand who I am."*
– Pat Schuler, patcoach@earthlink.net

10. Coaching is a platform from which to launch yourself, if desired.

When you learn the coaching skill set and take your personal and professional development to the next level, you will develop a local, regional,
national and even international reputation. Hundreds and thousands (even
tens of thousands) of people will know who you are or have been coached
or assisted by you. This popularity gives you many options – writing a
book, teaching TeleClasses, live trainings, e-newsletters, forming communi-
ties, getting business invitations from others and more.

Several Coach U graduates have recently published popular books. Oprah! featured Coach U graduate Laura Berman Fortgang, author of "Take Yourself to the Top: Secrets of America's #1 Career Coach". A successful personal coach and graduate of Coach U, Cheryl Richardson, wrote the best-selling "Take Time for Your Life".

Summing Up

Everyone has his or her own reasons for becoming a coach, but the ten benefits I've just outlined are enjoyed by almost every coach. The question to ask yourself is how YOU would benefit by becoming a coach.

Of all the benefits that come with being a coach, perhaps the most exciting benefit is the fact that you can select who YOU most want to work with. In other words, you can identify what we call your Ideal Client. What personality traits would they have? What kind of things do they want out of life? What past experiences have they had? What motivates them? What do they want to accomplish? What is most important to them?

Asking yourself these questions will help you know exactly who you can start coaching right away.

SECTION 4

WHY DOES A PERSON HIRE A COACH?

Most coaches do not advertise, yet many have a full practice. Why is this? Coaches are successful because people WANT to hire a coach and positive word of mouth attracts clients. Most people don't need to be sold on the idea of having their own coach – they either clearly see the value for themselves or they don't.

But you asked why a person hires a coach. Here are the most common reasons, with comments from actual clients of Coach U-trained coaches.

To set better goals.

The right goal – the goal that reflects your true values – is a joy to reach. The wrong goal – perhaps based on whims, advertising or instant gratification – takes needless effort and often comes at a high cost to you, your body and your soul. Coaches help people discover what they REALLY want, using the client's own values, needs and vision as personal reference points. They help clients eliminate the goals they've had forever that aren't really about them at all, but that they've always thought they "should" pursue.

> *"For the first time in my life I found myself without goals and was uncertain how to set goals for the next phase of my life. A supervisor suggested I work with a coach. With the help of my coach I have discovered who I really am. I am now making good decisions and setting goals that meet my needs, values and standards. I feel free and empowered!"*
> *– Kim Johnson, kimkj6@earthlink.net, www.nurse-watch.com*

To reach their goals faster.

Who doesn't want to reach their goals faster, especially if it is possible to reach their goals with less stress? The coach provides a consistent structure of support and offers innovative strategies and approaches to help clients reach their goals in record time. Coach U-trained coaches are familiar with Performance and Attraction Approach models and share these with their clients.

> *"People hire a coach to help them nurture the seed of greatness that lies dormant within them. They know it is there, but are not certain about the tools and methods to cultivate it. Coaching is about honoring and supporting the beliefs and individuality of each person so that they can grow and expand who they are in the way they want."*
> *– Amy Ruppert, amy@lightwork.net, www.lightwork.net*

> *"With my coach, I find myself addressing the 'source' of the problem instead of quick-fixing the 'symptoms.' This*

has lessened learning curves, created permanent solu-
tions and developed efficient systems thus contributing
to the overall growth of my individual businesses. I am
successfully avoiding making expensive mistakes."
– Entrepreneur, owner of multiple businesses (Client of
coach Jennifer Corbin, jennifer@compasscoaching.com,
www.compasscoaching.com

To make significant changes.

If you're human, you're making changes today, given the rapid rate of change in every aspect of life, business and technology. And if you're at all aware, you're making significant changes right now – or feel you could be. The coach is uniquely trained to help you make both fundamental and permanent changes in areas of your business, career, relationships and quality of life. You can even say that, with a coach, you will evolve yourself.

"While I underwent a significant career change, I relied
upon Sharon to help me focus, streamline and cele-
brate my transition. She is invaluable to me in more
areas of my life, now. I know whenever I have a signifi-
cant decision to make or life transition, I can rely upon
Sharon's wisdom, talent and humor to help me along
my life path."
– Greg Creech, former AT&T manager, current musi-
cian, speaker, artist, writer and blissful computer geek,
Pine Lake, Ga. (Client of Coach Sharon Day, sharon-
day@juno.com)

To become more financially successful.

Most clients want to either get started on a strong financial track or to build enough reserves in order to fund the life and lifestyle they want. Coaches are not financial planners, but they are knowledgeable about applying the concept of adding value, which is the source of financial independence for most individuals. A coach can also help you adjust your spending and lifestyle in order to better create your financial future.

"Why did I hire a coach? To become more financially
successful. I hired my coach after two consecutive
years of just breaking even in my law practice. During
the time we worked together, the bank required I pay
off my line of credit. Things looked bleak. Despite set-
backs, my coach helped me lay the foundation for long
term success through personal marketing and capacity
building. She even asked me to see the situation with
the bank as a good thing because it would lower my
debt. That was last year. This year I will end with over
$90,000 in profit and the prospects for next year are
even better. My coach made the difference."
– Anonymous client

To design – and live – the perfect life.

Is the perfect life possible today? Certainly. Every day, coaches help thousands of clients improve and perfect their life. It is part of our job and a source of our joy as coaches. Fortunately, clients are getting that they CAN have it all without paying the price. Coaches help them accomplish this.

> *"The value I received through my coaching sessions with my coach were many! With Sharon's encourage-ment, support and suggestions, I learned to slow down, prioritize the things in my life that were (and are) important to me and take GREAT care of myself. I've learned to ask for what I need and want, learned to say no and not feel guilty about it and decided to do the things I really wanted to do in my life! Sharon helped me to find and make the right changes in my life so that now I'm living the life I've always wanted!"*
> *– Sage Mueller, Professional Organizer, St. Louis, MO (Client of Coach Sharon Day, sharonday@juno.com)*

To get ahead professionally.

There are scores of ways to get ahead today in your career, profession or small business. The Coach U-trained coach knows the most effective career advancement strategies, reputation-building methods and business development tactics. Getting ahead has never been easier, with the right coach. Your coach is the consummate resource, because when you hire the right coach, you're tapping into their entire network of resources.

> *"I'm an artist working towards showing my works in a gallery. My coach and I work out the nitty-gritty details of what I need to do to achieve that goal each week, from taking photographs of my work to creating my bio. In spite of how I like things to be loose and not rigid, the structured way in which we do things has actually relieved me of stress and enhanced my creativity."*
> *– Nina Markman, Sculptor (Client of Coach Salila Shen, heartcoach@frontier.net)*

To make better decisions.

As life speeds up and as life becomes a smorgasbord, we are present-ed with far more choices than our parents ever were, but who had Decision-Making 101 in high school or college? Enter the coach, who can help you learn how to make the best decisions for YOU, regardless of the circumstances and even in the most confusing of situations. Coach U-trained coaches help clients make better decisions.

> *"You've really helped me see that the career I was torn about pursuing is just not what I really need to be doing with my life right now. For so long I have felt like 'I should do it,' or wondered 'Does God want me to do*

this?' But I know now that's not what I'm called to. I feel so free at last after coming to this decision. You've helped me clarify in a few months what I've been agonizing over for ten years. Finally I can see a glimmer of a way forward."
– Client of Coach Kathryn Andrew, mycoach@bigpond.com, www.users.bigpond.com/mycoach/

"When I approached Melinda to be my coach I thought I needed to change my job as the CFO of a non-profit organization. With Melinda's help I realized what I really needed was more time, space and joy. We used the 'Clean Sweep' to identify some 'improvement opportunities.' By eliminating some of the 'shoulds' and replacing them with 'wants,' I have found more peace and joy. And I discovered it wasn't my job that needed to change...it was me!"
– Linda K., CFO of a regional hospital foundation, client of Coach Melinda Vilas, mendycoach@aol.com

To have someone to collaborate with.

When you have someone to toss ideas around with, someone who understands the creative process, someone who expands your thinking, what you end up with is synergy. And, in our view, synergy is the bare minimum for success in the next decade. Without it, your creativity is limited; with it, creativity and innovation comes easily. The coach is a high-benefit, low-cost, no-obligation collaborative partner.

"I frequently use my coach as a focusing lens. I can bring a rough idea or concept to the session and just sort of start talking about it without concern for organization or logic. She uses her listening skills, experience and intuition to help me refine and focus the concept and to see different perspectives. This is a simple but rare resource for anyone who relies on his/her own creativity for success. This process alone has helped me to be well on the way to doubling my income in the next six months."
– Doug Hudiburg, dhudiburg@msn.com

To improve their relationships and family.

The more virtual the world gets, the more important your relationships and relationship skills become. Strengthening your family and attracting and maintaining friendships, colleague-ships and partnerships are key to providing meaning, support and love in your life. It's virtually impossible to be successful and fulfilled without the right people in your life. But as people work harder and as the world moves faster, people become disconnected and often find they've set relationships aside, then found themselves isolated and unhappy. Others look around and see that their relationships are one-way or lack the spark they crave. Your coach can help you improve your communication and relating skills and to attract the best people to you.

> *"My coach and I worked through her 101 point coaching program for attracting a fulfilling, lasting love. What I have created is a more fulfilling life, by learning how to identify my needs, ask for support when my needs are not being met and completing past relationships that stood in the way of my future ones. I am no longer a lone soul waiting for the perfect partner; now I know what I need in a partner and know I will attract him. Without the relationship coaching I would have remained in the same old patterns in my life, personal and professional and would not have been able to establish new relationship patterns."*
> *– Sloane Englert, sloane3@hotmail.com*

To make a bigger impact in the world.

Want to make your mark in this life or make a difference on the planet? People like you are working with coaches to identify their unique strengths and resources and to use these as a way to make a local or global difference, without the traditional high emotional or physical cost that comes with leadership.

> *"Coaching has been a blast of fresh air coming into thought processes about where you are going. It's given perspective, a positive way forward. My personal target is to save 500,000 pounds in two years. I see I can do it. The level of enthusiasm and communication in my company has increased. We now know we can achieve great things."*
> *– Owner of a London (UK) based international business consultancy*

To simplify their life.

Can you really have it all and yet simplify your life at the same time? Yes, absolutely. Coach U-trained coaches use a simple 3-step coaching model that helps a client to simplify, yet also enrich their life. It is one of the many proprietary methods and technologies that Coach U-trained coaches alone are licensed to use with clients.

> *"It seems like such a little thing but all those papers and disarray at home would really get me down at the end of each day. Now that I know I don't have to take my whole holidays to sort things out, but that I can 'action and file' three pieces of paper a day, I feel such an incredible sense of relief! And what's more amazing is I'm starting to get to the end already. I feel so much more on top of things and it's so great to be able*

to find things again. I never realized the impact this
had on the rest of my life."
– Client of Coach Kathryn Andrew, mycoach@big-
pond.com, www.users.bigpond.com/mycoach/

To strengthen their Personal Foundation.

It is impressive to see the number of clients coming to a coach with a
goal of strengthening themselves from the inside out. They do know that
external support and motivation is helpful, but also know that if they
strengthen who they are and what they have (called Personal Foundation),
they will have a much stronger and more resilient base from which to succeed. Coach U invented the term Personal Foundation and Coach U-
trained coaches may offer the Personal Foundation Program to their clients.

"When I began coaching, my life was in shambles. I
was single, had just been laid off my job, had no
friends, no support group, a house I could not sell and
bills pouring in the door. Then, at a conference, I met
Joanne and hired her to be my coach. With the help of
my coach, I turned myself inside out and upside down.
Joanne helped me to evaluate my life and determine
what I needed in my life to make me happy and to feel
complete. I ended up with four job offers, sold the
house, paid off huge chunks of bills. I now live in a
beautiful space that brings me peace, am making new
quality friends and may even have met my soul mate."
– Julia Larson, Resource Management, Charlotte, NC
(Client of Coach Joanne Ivancich,
coach4you@aol.com, www.LifeDesignInstitute.com)

To reduce stress and tolerations.

Stress comes with our times, but an increasing number of people recognize that the cost of this stress is too high and that it's not worth it. So,
they come to a coach who helps them to identify and reduce their personal
stress levels, benefiting their body, mind and spirit. Coach U-trained coaches also use the Toleration-Free approach as well. By identifying what you're
putting up with – and eliminating these - your stress level is instantly
reduced.

"Sometimes the session turns my whole week around."
– Tarra Guerra, Musician, Mother, College Professor
(Client of Nancy D. Simmons, NDSimmons@aol.com,
http://member.aol.com/ndsimmons/index.htm)

To increase income or revenue.

Seeking to get a raise or build your business? A coach can help by
helping you to craft a career or marketing strategy to do so. Coach U-
trained coaches have learned dozens of such strategies covering virtually
every aspect of personal income or business revenue enhancement.

"I have a sales and marketing background and tend to attract a lot of sales professionals as clients. It is so exciting to help already successful people double or triple their income and do so with less stress and more balance. Somewhere along the line, most salespeople were told that personal financial success always carries a high cost in other areas of life. Stress and feeling out of balance is thought to be just part of the game. In fact, the opposite is true. Bringing every aspect of the self into balance, practicing extreme self-care and building a strong personal foundation, all help to create the space for more success. You can have it all if you tend to the details and have the help of a coach."
– Doug Hudiburg, dhudiburg@msn.com

To become a better manager, executive or businessperson.

Many coaches are former managers, executives or business owners from virtually every field and industry. They can help you strengthen your management, leadership or entrepreneurial skills because they've been there or because they understand YOU.

"As a Dr. of Veterinary Medicine I've become concerned about the focus on the commercial side of running a practice. I feel that standards are slipping and that both Vets and Nurses are becoming slipshod in the care of animals. Since starting with my coach I've learned to stand back, to take more time with each patient and am making inroads in encouraging my staff colleagues to employ extreme care at all times. My boundaries are set - I will no longer allow myself to be hurried."
– Client of Coach Jilly Shaul, lifematters@btinternet.com

To become Internet-savvy.

Email and the Web are changing the world, and changing it very, very quickly. A growing number of clients are hiring coaches to help them make sense of the Internet, learn how to use it to market themselves or their business, establish web sites, offer virtual training services and/or host a worldwide community or network of their own. All Coach U-trained coaches are on the Internet and some of them specialize in it.

Summing Up...

As you've read, there are many good reasons to hire a coach, but you might be wondering how you can become a coach if you don't know all of the things described above.

There are two things you should know. First, Coach U will train you in all of the areas described above. We will give you the information, strategies and models referred to above. And, you CAN learn these. They are innovative and not difficult to learn. Second, clients hire you because you are YOU. Clients hire you because they feel that your personality, style, strengths and approach suits them.

No client expects you to be a master in all of the areas covered above, but they do expect you to at least be familiar with them.

Thanks to the comprehensive nature of the Coach U training, plus the extensive Reference Library and the web-based Coach U Knowledge base, you have exclusive access to everything we have on all of these subjects. This allows for just-in-time learning and lifelong reference, updated annually at no extra cost to you.

SECTION 5

HOW DOES A COACH WORK WITH CLIENTS?

Now that you know what a coach and client focus on, you might be wondering what the coach does for the client during a typical coaching session. In fact, we are often asked by those considering becoming a coach what they will actually DO with clients, and why that makes the coach worth $75 to $300 per hour to their clients. Here are the most common things that a coach does with a client, and why it matters.

A coach listens.

When is the last time when someone really listened to you and listened completely, so well and so perfectly that you both felt heard and also began seeing a solution or opportunity so clearly that you wonder why you hadn't seen it before? When a coach listens, they hear YOU, not just your current situation. And when YOU feel heard, you can hear yourself. That's worth a lot. As part of "Listening," an eight-week course in the training curriculum at Coach U, new coaches learn the ten most important listening skills and the 25 most important things to listen for. Through study, practice and feedback, they become highly attuned listeners who hear much more than is actually articulated.

> *"My job as a coach is to listen to words, but hear the energy – the feelings behind the words. This requires perception, intuition and above all, an openness to all of life. By this I mean, the coach can not be afraid of any of life's myriad feelings. If the coach is uncomfortable with sadness, for example, he or she won't be able to 'hear' the sadness in a client's words. As I have worked through and accepted my own feelings of anger, joy, sadness, disappointment, etc., I can easily feel them in clients' words. Once the feeling is acknowledged, any circumstance can be easily rectified. This is a tremendous service to the client."*
> *– David Buck, dave@davebuck.com,*
> *www.davebuck.com*

> *"Coaching provides an almost sacred space where my clients can safely tell the truth about their lives."*
> *– Pamela Richarde, peacecoach@innerspirit.com,*
> *www.innerspirit.com*

A coach lends support.

Does the Olympic skater attempt to win the gold medal by herself? No, she's smart enough to reach out and find the right coach who will bring out her best, because your own personal best is what makes life fulfilling, not to mention successful. In recent years, people have become very willing to reach out and ask for support while they make changes, solve problems or go for the gold. Asking for support is no longer a sign of weakness; it is a sign of intelligence. Through their training at Coach U, coaches learn how to provide extensive, customized and effective support to clients, without creating a dependency on the coach.

> *"I have accomplished so many profoundly important things as a direct result of working with my coach over the last two years. Our partnership was effective because of the way she applied her life experience, training and commitment to my highest good and expression of my highest potential. I have never felt support like this before."*
> *– Mariette Edwards (Client of Coach Barbara Hannah, barbara@lovinglife.net)*

A coach often challenges clients.

If you look back at your life, you can probably come up with the names of the three people who most challenged you to take a chance, invest in yourself or to make a big change. You may have felt stressed at the time, but are now grateful for the courage and care it took for those people to have challenged you to do things differently or just go for it. A coach does this for their clients, every day. Coaches want their clients to look back five years from now and say, "Wow, thank goodness my coach had the foresight to nudge me back then!" Coaching is an investment that pays off over a lifetime. Coaches at Coach U learn when, where and how to challenge their clients, for maximum long-term benefit. They also learn how to issue a challenge in such a way that the client feels both empowered to accept it and free to decline it or to counter-offer.

> *"I have been challenged to move out of my comfort zone. I was able to make a somewhat radical career shift in the last few months without any doubts or regrets, which has allowed me to significantly increase my income. Without all the changes I had made in the past year as a result of having a coach, I may not have had the right pieces (or mindset) to make the leap."*
> *– Jennifer O'Tool, Human Resources Product Consultant (Client of Coach Joanne Ivancich, Coach4you@aol.com, hwww.LifeDesignInstitute.com)*

A coach is motivational.

Humans being human and life being life, we all need help staying focused and motivated and the coach provides this as part of their service. Some clients want to be reminded of things, others need the occasional pep talk, others need encouragement and others prefer to be inspired. Whatever flavor of motivation the client needs, the coach can provide it. Remember, people who hire a coach are up to great things and encouragement is an important ingredient in their success. After all, we ARE human.

> *"I have always been an entrepreneur. It can be lonely at times. The coach I work with provides me the*

opportunity to be heard, to have a sounding board and
most of all he motivates me."
– Kathy Pike, kathyp@tesser.com,
www.CoachKPike.com

"In my entire 18 years in the software industry, no one
ever sent me a letter telling me I'd changed their lives
or that I was inspirational!"
– Pat Schuler, patcoach@earthlink.net

A coach guides the client.

Life used to be pretty simple because most people were provided a
career and lifestyle path and simply followed it – or fought it. But over the
past 30 years, it has dawned on us that there is no single correct path and
that we get to create this path for ourselves. Yet, where are we taught how
to create a path that's joyful, prosperous and balanced? That's where the
coach comes in. By learning about their client and helping the client to
discover what they most want personally and professionally, the coach can
offer the perspective, wisdom and reference points that help make a client's
life more fulfilling, successful and rewarding.

Coaches at Coach U receive extensive training in the life planning
process...and as a part of their training, they develop their own life plan,
which their individual coaches support them in living.

"Clients hire me as their coach to guide them in
designing the personal and professional life they desire.
Together we create plans, set goals, eliminate obsta-
cles, take chances and learn from each other along the
way. It's like guiding someone on a journey that they
have been waiting a long time to take because they
were hesitant to go alone."
– Dawn M. Osborn, M.S., Dawn@keys-to-
success.com, www.keys-to-success.com

A coach collaborates with clients.

Synergy is what occurs when two people collaborate and that's exactly
what coaches do with their clients. Coaches are active co-creators with
their clients, not just passive listeners. Most clients hire a coach whose
opinion, experience and accomplishments they respect and they expect the
coach to share their views on things affecting the client's personal and
professional life. In fact, many clients hire a coach because they want that
third eye, sounding board or creative partner to help the client achieve what
they most want, in the easiest, most enjoyable manner. As a coach, what
you say is as important as what you hear. Coaches at Coach U learn
advanced collaboration and creativity skills.

"Then there are the calls that begin with the client
saying, 'I don't know what to talk about today.' These
can be the best. We start to speak and the dialogue

often leads us to discover exciting new areas for investigation and accomplishment...something much more fruitful than a review of goals and actions taken. This can only happen when the coach and client are true collaborators and trust in the power of creativity."
– Jay Perry, Jay@CoachingCollective.com, www.CoachingCollective.com

A coach evolves his or her clients.

Humans are evolving, just like every other form of life. We may call it professional development, personal growth or transformation, but these are all part of our personal evolution. True, most clients don't walk in asking for personal evolution, but they do know they want to develop themselves in new ways, personally and professionally. As a coach, you can provide clients with the type of development or evolution that the client wants. And as a coach trained at Coach U, you may participate in the Personal Evolution Course, which will help you upgrade your environment so that it naturally evolves you and you'll then be able to coach your clients to do the same.

"Each time I speak with my coach, I am astonished and thrilled at how much detail she sees and remembers about me and my life. And the way she can pull an insight out of thin air, right in the moment, is astounding! Salila Shen is a magician! She can hear something in what I am saying and say it back to me in another way and it can completely change my life right then and there! I am gaining more from this relationship than I could ever have imagined. I look forward to every session wondering what 'aha!' will be uncovered next."
– Bhasa Leona Markman, Administrator, Santa Cruz, CA, USA (Client of Coach Salila Shen, heartcoach@frontier.net)

"My coach creates a space where there is no place for me to hide. I get to see myself exactly as I am. And from there, I am encouraged to move forward."
– Steve Davis, davissm@ridgenet.net

A coach asks powerful questions.

One of the best ways to provide value to a client is to ask the right question at the right time in the right manner. In fact, we call these Lazer Questions – fundamental questions that cut to the core of the matter and get the client thinking bigger and thinking better. A single question – if it's the right one – can be worth tens of thousands of dollars to a client. Every coach at Coach U gets a list of the 100 most effective Lazer Questions and learns to gracefully use those that are most appropriate in the moment.

"With the simplest yet most pertinent of questions, my coach transformed my life from a bunch of 'shoulds' to

a path that is right for me. The life-changing question: 'What in your life, that you think you do out of love and support, is really because you are scared of losing control?' Powerful stuff!"
– Wendy Buckingham, classone@zeta.org.au

A coach understands.

The coach is expected to be both understanding – meaning patient, caring and respectful of the client – as well as be a professional who understands the dynamic of virtually any situation, problem or choice that a client is facing. The client is paying for a coach's wisdom and insight. And the client wants to work with a coach who can help them make sense of what's going on, because once the coach accurately assesses and explains the situation, the client is free to start working on a solution. Isn't it a terrific skill to be able to KNOW what's really going on in virtually any situation and to be able to help another person see it clearly? Coaches at Coach U learn how to coach a client in any of the 75 most common client situations.

> *"Choosing just-the-right coach is like choosing a dance partner - I needed someone with the same sense of rhythm and pace as me. I wanted a partner who could understand how I think and anticipate the next step. My coach likes working with highly motivated people like myself and understands what limits me. Coach U coaches come with such diverse backgrounds and unique styles, it is easy to find one that is just right as a partner."*
> *– Jane Yousey, ReachnHigh@aol.com*

A coach strategizes.

One of the roles of a coach is that of strategist. Basically, you help the client to identify the best and easiest way to accomplish something or to solve a problem. In other words, you help the client to answer the question, How will I achieve that?

It might surprise you to know that there are only about 30 strategies that a coach needs to know in order to be an effective strategist. Once you learn these strategies, you can help a client use one or more of them effectively in virtually any client situation.

Knowing your strategies gives you a competitive advantage in the marketplace, because it makes your coaching that much more effective and practical.
Coaches at Coach U take a course called "Strategizing," where they learn how to strategize with clients and are taught all 30 Situational Strategies.

> *"Wherever I am, whatever my dilemma, my coach seems to have the capacity to understand, without judgment, just what is going on and give me the right strategy to handle it cleanly and elegantly."*
> *– Wendy Buckingham, classone@zeta.org.au*

Summing up...

Coaching is really an advanced form of relating. Thus, a coach develops scores of specialized listening, communication and relating skills that they use to help a client identify what they want, clarify who they are and develop a strategy to reach their goals.

There is no mystery to the coaching process, but it does take about two years to master the professional skill set of coaching. If that sounds like a long time, it's because you not only learn the skill itself, but you also evolve yourself internally in order to deftly use the skill with a wide range of clients. Coaching is a sophisticated process and clients expect their coaches to thoroughly understand how to use their skills.

SECTION 6

WHAT TOOLS DO COACHES USE IN THEIR WORK?

Every profession has its own set of tools and specialized knowledge. For example, an accountant uses a calculator and accounting software, a chiropractor uses his hands and knowledge of the body and an optometrist uses lenses and other optical equipment. So, it makes sense that coaches have their own set of tools as well. The most common coaching tools are:

1. Self-assessment checklists.

Most clients want to learn more about themselves and better understand who they are and how they operate in life. Coach U has developed a series of over 20 self-assessments that coaches can share with clients. The available list is growing and includes assessments to help clients: discover and fulfill their personal needs, unlock and orient around their true values, accelerate their personal development, identify and eliminate conditions they're suffering from, strengthen their Personal Foundation, identify and treat the sources of business problems, prioritize, identify and leverage their strengths and more. The more the client learns about her/himself, the more she/he will benefit from coaching.

> *"The self-assessments give my clients a concrete platform for assessing their strengths and evaluating their progress in measurable ways. They give clarity and direction and a starting point for seeing the truth about themselves more clearly. These tests shorten the time it takes to get a baseline so that a client can use more of their energy in taking the actions that will make a difference."*
> *– Judy Godinez, judyg110@aol.com*

2. Client programs.

Close to 100,000 individuals have been coached by Coach U-trained coaches and over the years, we've been able to develop programs for individuals and businesses. Some programs are in the format of 100 point checklists such as New Business Start Up or SuperReserve Program. Others are packaged as learning modules/books such as The Attraction Program or Personal Foundation. In any case, these Client Programs can provide a template for the coach and a path for the client. In other words, with these programs, the coach doesn't need to reinvent the wheel. Also, these programs are terrific marketing tools as well.

> *"I think Coach U's Clean Sweep is just the best little self-assessment to give folks a quick, but deadly accurate, snapshot of just how 'together' their lives really are."*
> *– Judith E. Craig, Ph.D., judi@drcraig.com,*
> *www.drcraig.com, www.coachsquared.com*

3. Success Principles.

Most clients want to learn more about themselves and how to become more successful. Given this, the properly trained coach has at his or her disposal a comprehensive collection of what we call Success Principles. When the coach learns these and integrates them into their own knowledge base, they have that much more to offer clients.

> *"My vision is to CO-ACHieve success. The greatest gift that I can give my clients is the power and the strength to need me for nothing."*
> *– Keith Collins, Keith@incondition.freeserve.com.uk, www.coachreferral.com/coaches/c/collins1001910.html*

> *"Coach U offers coaches a concrete set of principles that I use in helping my career clients achieve success. These principles are invaluable in moving clients to higher levels of success. The principles are so well-detailed that coaches can listen for which principle a client needs. Then, coaching programs accelerate the application of the principle and significantly raise the level at which the client functions."*
> *– Marjorie Wall Hofer, leadercoach@usa.net*

4. Coaching Models.

Building on the Success Principle idea, Coach U has developed dozens of Coaching Models on virtually every aspect of the coaching process, as well as the most common situations in which clients find themselves. Most clients find it helpful to see a visual display of the situation or strategy and with this collection of Coaching Models, the coach can help the client to reach their goals much more quickly. Two of the most popular models are the 3-step Coaching Model and the S-5 Model (Situation>Symptom>Source>Solution>Shift).

> *"Listening is the pivotal skill of the coach. But how does one listen and measure the effectiveness of that listening? The S-5 model we teach at Coach U – situation-symptom-source-solution-shift – represents a breakthrough for fully understanding the client situation and propelling them past the obstacles in their path toward their objective. At each juncture (aka 's' in the model), coaching opportunities abound. I found this model to be equally effective coaching CEOs, entrepreneurs, professionals in private practice, individuals in transition and any other type of client who embraces coaching. It is a sorely overlooked way of relating, in my estimation. If I didn't use a single other model with clients, I believe I would serve them splendidly if I relentlessly, religiously and committedly coached from this orientation."*
> *– Meryl Moritz, urbancowgirl@worldnet.att.net*

Summing Up...

As you can see, coaching is a lot more than just motivating and supporting your clients. There is a technology and methodology to coaching. The process is easily learnable because you first become familiar with the tools that a coach uses. Once you are familiar with the coach's toolbox, you learn coaching skills.

HOW DOES A COACH FIND CLIENTS?

While not everyone who becomes a coach wants to develop a coaching practice (because many coaches work for a company or wish to use the coaching methods and skills in their current professions), most coaches do develop a practice. And of all the questions we answer each year from prospective coaches, we are most often asked, "How can I find clients?" Over the past 10 years, Coach U has perfected the art of practice development and it includes the following key components. Given that advertising and cold calling rarely works to find clients, we suggest you focus on the proven, relationship-based methods of finding clients.

Here are 5 ways (of the 100 ways we've identified) to build your coaching practice:

1. Expand your referral network.

They say that – from a marketing perspective – you are worth the value of your network, squared. In other words, if you have/know 100 people in your personal or professional network, your marketing value is $10,000 (100 x 100). And if you know (or are known by) 1,000 people, your value is $1,000,000 (1,000 x 1,000). Who knows if this equation is provable, but it does illustrate the value of having as many people in your network as possible, especially in today's world of inter-connectedness?

Networking today is a popular and acceptable skill set and as a coach you will benefit by expanding the number of people in your network. Because once you expand your personal and professional network, there are that many more people who know who you are, what you do and what you offer.

Dozens of socially acceptable ways of building your network to a "critical mass" have been developed. These techniques work even if you are not the most gregarious person you know.

When you have enough people in your network, the phone rings with referrals. It is as simple as that. After all, wouldn't you rather respond to business coming to you than trying to push people to hire you as a coach?

Two of the most effective ways to increase and strengthen your network are to use the Team 100 Checklist and the Jane Smart Letter.

The Team 100 Checklist

We have developed a list of 100 types of other professionals, such as attorneys, bankers, plumbers and the like. People just like you, except that they are in a different profession. We have even included this checklist in the Appendix of this book to get you started.

Using the checklist, you (or any client) will compile a list of everyone you know who fits into one of the professions listed on the form. Then, simply call each person to let him or her know what you do. Not to sell them on you, coaching or your services, but rather to tell them what you do, whom you do it for and how people benefit from your coaching services.

In other words, these calls are courtesy calls, not selling calls. Coaches in Coach U's training program even learn great ways of explaining what coaching is and smart answers to questions that the person you're speaking with may ask.

Obviously, you may first want to call the professionals that you already know or do business with. But soon, you'll have the confidence to ask them for professionals they know, but who you don't have yet on your list of 100. It takes about 90 days (at only 30 minutes a day) to complete the Team 100 checklist.

The Jane Smart Letter

Petrified to pick up the phone? No problem. You can use what we call the Jane Smart letter (yes, Jane Smart is a hypothetical coach whose name we made up, but by now we like her so well, we think we'll keep calling it that). Basically, this is a letter of self-introduction that you can send, fax or email to as many people as you have in your Rolodex. It's creatively and professionally worded to not be a sales pitch, but rather to explain what coaching is and outline exactly what you are doing with clients. The Jane Smart Letter works very, very well, because it is not a typical intro or promotional letter. And it is customizable to fit your target market. We've included one version of it in the Appendix.

By ensuring that at least one hundred professionals and people in your network know exactly what you do, you'll spark your referral engine. You're on your way to filling your practice, without having to sell anyone anything. It's clean, its quick and it consistently works.

> *"In January 1999, I moved my company to another state. Because my network was strong and because I keep them well-informed of the news in my practice and life, they celebrated my move and still know where to find me. When I moved, I did not lose touch with the people who send me referrals, nor did it become any harder for them to send me business."*
> *– Barbara Hannah, barbara@lovinglife.net*

2. Coach 100 people, for free if necessary.

Part of being a great coach is recognizing when people around you can benefit from your time, encouragement, advice or presence. One of the strategies that successful coaches use is something simple called generosity. In other words, when you see a need, you offer to help, whether you get paid for it or not.

Now, if you already have a professional practice and a strong reputation in your current field, you may not need or want to be as generous as I am suggesting. But if you don't have coaching clients or you want to transition your current practice to include coaching, then please listen up.

I'm not saying you should be so generous as to have a full practice of non-paying clients, but I am suggesting that you seek to serve instead of seek to sell. It's a huge shift and leap of faith to take your focus off building your coaching revenue and instead concentrate on being generous with your time and resources. Again, though, the most successful coaches have gotten that way by coaching anyone and everyone they could in order to build experience and build a referral engine.

It's fair to say that you already know at least 25 people who could benefit from your coaching. And most of them aren't yet aware of it. But as a coach, you know it. And that means that you have the advantage. You have something they can benefit from, you're willing to give it to them and all they have to do is agree that it's a good idea and say yes. Hey, offering coaching is not rocket science.

Not sure how to help these individuals you have earmarked? No problem. Just ask them how you can help. Really. In other words, if you sense they could use some help, support or advice, yet don't know what exactly they need from you, just ask them. They WILL tell you and your coaching relationship will be off and running, without you having to sell yourself or coaching. All you have to do is to sell the person on THEMSELVES and what THEY want and coaching will sell itself.

> *"The first trick about becoming a coach is go out and coach people. Coach your friends, your family and your neighbors and for free if necessary. Get some experience and then one day you will get a call, 'You don't know me but...' Congratulations! You just got your first paying client!"*
> *– Gavin Ingham, gavin@harvest.freeserve.co.uk*

3. Start an E-Newsletter

One of the most successful ways to build a practice – and keep it full – is to start an electronic newsletter. Pick a topic, perhaps your specialty or a personal or business topic that would appeal to your ideal clients. Start sending out your e-newsletter every week or two to people who want to subscribe to it. You can even make it a daily tip if you wish. Tens of millions of individuals on the Internet subscribe to these free e-newsletters.

As you build your subscriber base, you'll find that about 1-5% of them will either become clients, refer clients to you or will take a TeleClass you offer. That might not sound like a very high ratio, but remember, an e-newsletter takes the same amount of energy regardless of the number of subscribers. Build your base and you've got an effortless marketing engine purring away for you. We call this type of marketing Capillary Marketing because you are sending out good content to people all over the world that want to receive it. You cannot predict exactly what comes back to you, but clients WILL come to you as a result. This is a proven method. Depending on your topic, it will take between 6-12 months to build your subscriber base to about 1,000 which is where you should start seeing some clients out of it. Not a writer? Coaches at Coach U can access the Coach U collection of over 10,000 knowledge nuggets on 50 subjects (see Appendix for a list of topics), and include or adapt some of these for your daily or weekly broadcast. If you don't like the idea of selling your coaching services to people around you, then this Capillary Market Method is your best bet because it attracts clients to you.

> *"I was skeptical at first about whether writing my own newsletter would be worth the effort. I decided to give*

*it a shot and boy has it been worth it! After sending
just three issues of the newsletter, I received a phone
call from someone who had attended my workshop
several months before. After reading the newsletter
articles she realized that she was just not reaching her
goals on her own. She was ready to hire me and
wanted to know how to get started.*

*I was also unsure about whether or not I could develop
a large enough subscriber base to make my newsletter
viable. You can imagine my excitement when I discovered the dramatic power of the forward button! I started with about 250 people and in less than six months I
had nearly 850 subscribers. Writing my own newsletter
had allowed me to leverage other people's networks.
People who I never would have met on my own receive
my newsletter and they, too, forward my articles to
people in their networks."
– Joanne Ivancich, coach4you@aol.com,
www.LifeDesignInstitute.com*

4. Improving Your Life

Can you get new clients just by improving your own life? Yes! The
happier you are and the more proud you are about the quality of your own
life, the better you'll feel about telling people that you are a coach. We recommend that coaches first start with the Clean Sweep Program, which is
included in the Appendix. This is a 100-point checklist that will guide you
through the life improvement process in 4 primary areas of your life:
Relationships, Physical Environment, Money and Well-Being. As you
increase your score on this checklist, you'll naturally attract clients.

*"I enrolled in Coach U to become a professional coach.
I never realized it would have such an immediate
impact on the quality of my life. I have gotten rid of tol-
erations, identified needs and values, solidified my own
Personal Foundation, become more attractive...and so
much more. And the best part is that by improving the
quality of my own life, I have become a better coach!"
– Renee Lanman, ReneeLan@aol.com*

Summing Up...

Most new coaches are concerned about their ability to attract enough
clients to build a vibrant practice, so the five client-development strategies
above should provide some peace of mind. At Coach U, we know that
finding clients is extremely important and we do more than any professional-
training school we know of to give you every marketing tool and strategy to
fill your practice.

THE COACH U APPROACH™

By now, you've probably got a good feeling for whether becoming a coach is the right thing for you right now. In this section, I would like to describe the special approach that Coach U uses in its training of coaches. You'll read about our philosophy, our effective system of training coaches, the unique culture at Coach U, the coaching methodology we teach and who enters Coach U.

How does Coach U train coaches?

Coach U has developed an innovative system for training coaches to be highly effective. In fact, we call it the Coach U Approach™. Here is how and why it works so well.

1. Having the Right Colleagues

You learn how to coach well by surrounding yourself with coaches as eager to learn as you are. It's probably not politically correct to say so, but there are not only different styles among coaches, but also a varying quality of coaches. In other words, not all coaches are fully trained and not all coaches take the time to master their craft. So, it's important to put yourself into a community of coaches who ARE personally committed and intellectually able to master this craft. Just like a computer has to have lots of RAM and a fast CPU, so do coaches, given the pace and complexity of our clients lives, goals and needs. One of the things you'll find at Coach U is a student body eager and able to learn. They know this is a rich profession and that it is worth learning the skills, concepts and strategies properly.

> *"Being a part of Coach U is the equivalent of wandering in the desert for years and suddenly finding your tribe. People who are interested in the same outcomes for life, speak the same language and are committed to improving life for themselves and those they encounter."*
> *– Cynthia Bahnuik, cbahnuik@incentre.net*

> *"Coach U and the culture of coaching is truly international. There is no finer way to become a citizen of the world than to cultivate these friendships in every corner of the globe."*
> *– Keith Collins, Keith@incondition.freeserve.com.uk, www.coachreferral.com/coaches/c/collins1001910.html*

2. Using the 3-Step Coaching Model

You learn how to coach well by starting with the 3-step Universal Coaching Model™ and the coaching process. As complex as clients can be, the coaching process is fairly simple, albeit rich. Coach U invented the Universal Coaching Model methodology and it is the easiest to learn and most powerful coaching model available today.

In our view, the coaching process is about:
1. Helping the client to discover and understand who he or she is;
2. Helping the client identify and clarify what he or she most wants;
3. Helping the client to create and develop strategies for how he or she will achieve goals.

In our view, what makes coaching coaching is the 'who' part. Goals (what) and strategies (how) are terrific, but unless they are integrated with the person (who), they will take longer to accomplish, will probably not be what the person really wants and certainly will not bring the high levels of happiness and fulfillment that are possible.

What's powerful about the Universal Coaching Model is that it's not linear. Depending on the client, you can start at any of the three portals (who, what or how), and you can weave your way through all three of them, as needed, during the coaching process.

Obviously, there is a lot more to this model. We have identified the 25 extensions for each of the three areas (who, what and how) and these provide the basis for the Coach Training Program.

> *"What are the results? Vision, clarity, peace, happiness, joy, simplicity, beauty, love, spirituality, synchronicity, abundance, creativity and understanding. So much has happened to me throughout this process, it is difficult to capture in words. Those who know me comment on my aura of happiness, my clarity about finally seeing who I am, what I want, how to get it and what I have to offer the world."*
> *– Nancy Kindler, Marketing Specialist, Edmonton, Alberta, Canada (Client of Coach Cynthia Bahnuik, cbahnuik@incentre.net)*

3. Understanding People

You learn how to coach well by learning over 100 things about humans, including what motivates us, how we operate and what it takes to be successful in life. Specifically, a coach knows about personal needs, the seven stages of development, developmental accelerators, the reduction of resistance, the role of environments, core values, sources of motivation, cultural differences, belief systems, assumptions/expectations and genetic/memetic drivers. It's safe to say that you will also learn a lot about yourself in the process of learning about people. And the better you come to understand yourself, the easier it becomes to coach others effectively.

> *"When people ask me if becoming a coach and attending Coach U has been worthwhile, I always respond with, 'Even if I never coach another person in my life, the training and all that I have learned about myself and about what makes people tick has been so tremendous. That alone makes it worthwhile.'"*
> *– Lucinda Kerschensteiner, lucindak@prodigy.net*

4. Coaching Others Right Away

You learn how to coach well by coaching others within the first 90 days of entering Coach U. Given that most of the coaches at Coach U already have some experience in working with others in a managerial or advisory capacity, we suggest that you work with clients just as soon as you would like to. The curriculum is designed to provide you with enough fundamentals of coaching and enough coaching tools to be able to coach fairly well from the very beginning. With time – and training and experience – you'll become masterful. Some coaches are hesitant to start coaching until they understand it all, but our view is that as long as your client knows and is comfortable with your current expertise/experience level, then its okay to coach as soon as you wish. Further, you'll never become masterful without practice, so you'd better dive right in! You can wait if you wish, but you will get more out of your coach training if you are working with between 5 and 25 clients.

"I thought that I would begin coaching others when I completed the Coach U program. I now understand that becoming a coach means being one. It means coaching others right away. I realized that I tend to learn more by participating personally versus simply observing. I retain more by applying things than just reading a text. The quickest way to become a Master coach is by having clients."
– Renee Lanman, ReneeLan@aol.com

5. Being Coached Yourself

You learn how to coach well by being coached yourself. Most coaches work with a Mentor Coach or a buddy coach. A Mentor Coach is a coach who has a track record of mentoring new coaches. A buddy coach is a friend or colleague that you coach and who coaches you, for free. By having your own coach, you'll quickly discover what you like and don't like in the coach's style and that accelerates your own training process.

"Learning to become a coach without having a mentor coach seems like pushing a car uphill! I have had a mentor coach from my third month at Coach U and she has supported me through thick and thin and really helped me hone my skills. I learn from her what works for me, then turn around and use that with my own clients. It's also been really helpful to discuss better ways of coaching my new clients."
– Kathryn Andrew, mycoach@bigpond.com,
www.users.bigpond.com/mycoach/

6. Learning by Listening to Masters

You learn how to coach well by listening to the best coaches coach via TeleClass, RealAudio or audiotape. As many coaches as you can listen to as they coach, the better. This, because some of the advanced coaching techniques cannot be taught, but you CAN learn them, by listening and observing.

> *"The level of personal development and life mastery is evident in many of the TeleClass leaders and associates at Coach U. The open sharing of information, experiential knowledge and support demonstrated by the Coach U masters has been a larger part of my education at Coach U. Modeling after the masters at Coach U alone has been worth the tuition."*
> *– Kathy Pike, kathyp@tesser.com,*
> *http://www.CoachKPike.com*

In addition to the TeleClass leaders each coach meets and interacts with, coaches in training enjoy learning from master coaches via audiotape. Coach U has developed over 500 hours of audiotapes of masterful coaches coaching. Students at Coach U can listen to all of these tapes via RealAudio at no additional charge. The real-time coaching tapes are organized by client type and situation, so you learn both different styles of coaching as well as learn how to coach specific types of clients.

> *"I'm loving the new coaching audio set. I drove 800 miles in the last two days and it was actually delightful!!! I listened to tapes the entire way. I was so engrossed at one point that I actually ran out of gas! Fortunately, I was near a gas station and would you believe I was so pumped by the excitement of listening to the tapes that I was only mildly concerned about running out of gas and that was because it was interfering with my 'lazer coaching sessions.'"*
> *– Kim Collard Worlow, worlow@mtnhome.com*

7. Tapping into the Coach U Knowledge Base

You learn how to coach well by referring to The Reference Library when you need help with a specific client or situation. We have identified the 75 most common client types and 75 more common client situations and these are available for searching and viewing at the student-only area of the Coach U website (http://www.coachu.com). So, the next time you have, let's say, an entrepreneur client who keeps shooting himself in the foot, you can get some helpful coaching strategies and tips on your various options. The Library also contains assessments, client management forms and guidelines, marketing tools, coaching skills and client programs. A complete list of the Library contents is located in the Appendix.

> *"I believe that Coach U is committed to providing the finest resources available for creating an extraordinary coaching practice. Coach U's programs and materials are designed to empower each student in discovering what you truly value most in coaching."*

8. Participating in TeleClasses
You learn how to coach well by participating in TeleClasses from senior coaches on virtually every aspect of coaching and every type of client. As part of your coach training, you participate in up to 200+ hours of TeleClasses. A TeleClass is a conference call, so all you need is a regular telephone; you can call to your classes from anywhere in the world. Our conferencing system is located in the U.S. The TeleClasses are an extremely effective way to learn because each class has a single focus, is conducted by a coach who knows that subject area and is collaborative in nature. Every coach on the call discusses the key points of the class, with ample time to bring case studies and client situations to the table for group input as well as advice and wisdom from the instructor. A complete list of TeleClasses currently offered at the time of printing is located in the Appendix, but new classes on cutting-edge topics such as group coaching and Irresistible Attraction are added regularly.

61

"Participating in the TeleClasses at Coach U has allowed me to gain insights and new ideas that have helped me to be a better coach. Interacting with people in different professions, from other countries, of different age groups and with different interests and life experiences has helped me to broaden my knowledge base and pass this on to others."
– Dawn M. Osborn, M.S., Dawn@keys-to-success.com, www.keys-to-success.com

"I am finding the content of the TeleClasses to be a wonderful 'help for life' in a number of areas as well as great coaching instruction. With subjects like Listening, Relating, Cyberskills, etc., I feel I am getting the best training possible."
– Marilyn Hall, halls@intur.net

9. Using Coaching Programs with Clients
You learn how to coach well by practicing with Client Programs that you can use immediately with clients. There are times when you coach a client intuitively based on what they need during that coaching session. The client tells you what's going on and you respond to what they ask for. But there are other times, when the client wants more structure and focus. Then, what they really want is a program of some type that fits for their situation, style or profession. For example, a client starting a new business usually wants help creating and implementing a plan, but they also want to make sure they aren't forgetting anything. The solution? The New Business Start Up Program. Or how about a client who wants to strengthen or improve their life in every area – from their stress level to time management; from boundaries-extension to standards-raising, from toleration-

reduction to personal organization... and do it quickly! The solution? The Personal Foundation Program. Coach U has developed over 40 such programs that you can use and share with individual clients, with no royalty required. Some clients prefer the framework of a client program; other clients do not. It's important to be able to serve clients by having access to these proven programs.

> *"My clients usually have one or two of the Coach U programs running 'in the background,' even if we don't talk about them each week. It's truly magical to complete one of the assessments, put it aside and return to it sometime later. Clients often find that their scores improve even without a lot of conscious effort. My feeling is that the assessments are so simple and so powerful that they resonate with people at a sub-conscious level. Taking the assessment subtly draws energy and attention to areas that need improvement, so those areas improve effortlessly. The process can be accelerated by conscious effort and coaching, but tends to roll along on its own once the attention and intention exist."*
> *– Doug Hudiburg, dhudiburg@msn.com*

10. Developing Yourself

You learn how to coach well by developing and evolving yourself along the way. The title of this book is "Becoming a Coach." It's not "Doing Coaching." What I mean to say is that being a great coach is one part skill development and one part personal development. After all, you're not a coaching service. What you are is a coach. And, your clients are hiring YOU, not your coaching service. In other words, the more you develop yourself as you develop your skills and abilities, the more attractive you will be to the best clients. It's fair to say that most of the coaches who enter Coach U have already been developing themselves personally for some time. They've taken classes, read books, cultivated a spiritual practice and simply sought growth through their experiences. They are already on a personal development track. But at Coach U you will accelerate your progress on your path and also leap on to the process of Personal Evolution, which is the next stage of personal development.

> *"'...life used to be so ha-a-ard... Now every-thing is easy 'cause of youuu.' Crosby, Stills, and Nash weren't singing about Personal Foundation in the 60's but I wish they had been. Coach U's notion of being healthfully selfish and building a strong foundation has made most of my life extremely easy. Now if I want more out of life, I just strengthen my foundation and open wide to see what surprises the universe will send me next."*
> *– Jay Perry, Jay@CoachingCollective.com,*
> *www.CoachingCollective.com*

Summing Up...

So, now you know how we train the finest coaches in the world. If our approach suits you, we would love to have you enter Coach U.

SECTION 9

WHAT ARE THE ADVANTAGES OF ENROLLING IN COACH U?

As you've seen, this book describes the Coach U Approach™ to both coaching and to coaching training. Many people looking for coach training want to know the unique advantages of being a part of Coach U. This section details those advantages, enjoyed by both students of Coach U and those who've already graduated.

1. The Comprehensive, Inclusive Approach

There isn't a single approach that works for everyone. In fact, we know of a variety of approaches, strategies and paths to success. We teach all of them in the Coach Training Program, so that you can offer a complete menu to your clients. This way, you're able to customize your coaching to fit exacting client needs and preferences.

Coaches come from all backgrounds and have different cultural and style preferences. The Coach U Approach™ is sensitive to this cultural diversity and is also very illuminating as you learn how to effectively coach individuals from all walks of life and from every region in the world.

> *"The concepts and content of Coach U are truly awesome. They're still being expanded at a phenomenal pace! Luckily, one must master only a small percentage of the tools available to become a good coach and a great person. Coach U is a lifelong journey, not a degree course."*
> *– Keith Collins, Keith@incondition.freeserve.com.uk, www.coachreferral.com/coaches/c/collins1001910.html*

2. Just-In-Time-Learning Convenience

Coaches want to learn what they need to learn when they want to learn it and Coach U's flexible approach to TeleClass scheduling and use of RealAudio and self-study materials makes this possible. For example, say a Generation X-type client wants to work with you on building their business. You know a lot about building a business, but do you know a lot about how Generation Xers need to be treated and coached? Within minutes, you can review our class notes on this client type and listen to several GenXers tell you how they prefer to be coached.

Think of the time this just-in-time approach will save you, not to mention how it will improve the quality of your coaching because you learn exactly how to coach the client type you are working with. The Coach U System has also identified 50+ Client Types and Client Situations that you can access 24 hours a day via the exclusive student-only area of the Coach U website. You won't find this type of resource anywhere else.

> *"As an adult educator, I know the importance of real-time training. Many of my students over the years have told me that they were very excited in class, but lost*

*their zest for incorporating the principles learned once
they returned to the 'real world.' Coach U teaches
principles as they are needed so coaches can incorporate the principles into their work, fully embrace them
and see all the supporting and related principles.
What's more, the program is wonderfully time-flexible.
With four young children and a consulting business, I
need a program where, at night after the children are in
bed, I can pick up the phone and be in class."*
– Marjorie Wall Hofer, leadercoach@usa.net

3. A Flexible Professional Path

Some coaches want to coach full-time; others want to coach part-time
or to integrate the coaching skills and strategies they learn at Coach U into
their current job or business. Others start out with one path in mind, but
change their mind when they find a better one. Any way you want to use
your coaching skills, you can do so, thanks to the flexibility of the Coach
Training Program.

Want to get through the program quickly, perhaps even within one year?
No problem – take as many classes as you feel you can handle. Want to
take your time and complete the program at your own pace, say within three
or four years? No problem, take as much time as you like. Want to pick and
choose your classes based on immediate needs? Fine. Want us to recommend a learning track for you? We're happy to. You are a lifetime member
of Coach U and entitled to move at a pace that suits YOU.

Want to take the summer off and come back strong in the Fall? Hey,
summers are great – take time off if you like. Prefer to take your classes in
the morning one month and in the evenings another month? No problem.
TeleClasses are offered almost 24 hours a day. So, even if you're calling from
Europe, Hong Kong or London, you will find live TeleClasses available to you.

*"I looked at various courses when I discovered coach-
ing but none of them approached the professionalism
of Coach U, either in their approaches or in their raw
material. As for the flexibility, where else can you study
at the prestigious level of Coach U while taking courses
whenever you want and at your own pace?"*
– Gavin Ingham, gavin@harvest.freeserve.co.uk

4. Leading Edge Information and Tools

Freshness is very important to us at Coach U – you wouldn't buy stale
bread from your market; don't buy stale information from a training program.
We add both new content to the Coach U knowledge base and upgrade
current content to make sure its still relevant in a changing business and
personal world.

Over the past five years, the amount of materials available to students
and alumni at Coach U has increased at a rate of 100% per year. Each and
every year, we add new client programs, coaching models, TeleClasses,
audiotapes, marketing tools/techniques, business concepts, Internet

resources and published books. In fact, students and graduates of Coach U help us to expand and keep the inventory fresh.

We also read a lot ourselves, subscribe to the most progressive magazines (Fast Company, Business 2.0 and Wired) and test our new programs via the clients of the Coach U R&D Team Members. We ARE an intellectual factory. Our annual R&D budget runs about 18% of revenues, which is extremely high for a school and something of which we are very, very proud. Our materials are fresh, better, effective, learnable and teachable.

> *"One of the challenges of being a really good coach is staying on the leading edge of innovation and change. Coach U is a catalyst for continuous learning by focusing on new trends through visionary eyes and creating new courses and material, freely made available to members, to prepare coaches today to address the needs of tomorrow."*
> *– Brenda Thibault, brenda.thibault@wd.gc.ca*

5. Worldwide Network of Coaches

The fact that Coach U hosts a worldwide network of coaches is perhaps only an interesting feature to coaches entering Coach U.   But within a year or so, coaches realize how very powerful this community of coaches is, and how beneficial it is to be part of the Coach U Worldwide Network of Coaches.

As a coach at Coach U, you have over 3800 coaches to refer to and who can refer to you. You have thousands of specialists you can turn to for help with a client. And you have that many more people to connect with, benefit from and enjoy. Both professional and personal relationships result from this network. There have even been several marriages!

But the real value of being a part of the Coach U Network of Coaches is best shared by our Network members themselves:

> *"I still find it amazing to live on this island outside of Stockholm and be part of a global network and training effort in a new field. And it impresses my clients too."*
> *– Soren Holm, soren@utveckling.nu*

> *"There are very few if any other organizations that embody the spirit of sharing, caring and support that Coach U embodies.   If you need help on anything you can send out the call to anyone in the community and be deluged with responses. The community of Coach U is wonderful and still unbelievable at times it is so great."*
> *– Cynthia Bahnuik, cbahnuik@incentre.net*

> *"Enrolling at Coach U involved me in a terrific community of coaches! There are literally hundreds of coaches available through telephone or email. Their willingness to interact and share experiences is great! I have found*

*visiting with them to be a way to exchange ideas,
express feelings and concerns in a safe environment,
receive support, etc. From my initial inquiry about
Coach U to my current status as a busy student, it has
been like having a group of tour guides and mentors to
help me along."*
– Marilyn Hall, halls@intur.net

*"I have always been global-minded and have belonged
to numerous global organizations in the past. I was
overjoyed to realize that the coaching community is so
vast that it now covers the whole globe. What a wonderful sense of community. What a wonderful experience to be part of it."*
– Michael Sheffield, mscoach@sonic.net

*"It is very difficult to describe how very valuable it is to be
connected to the community at Coach U. The TeleClass
leaders, students and volunteers are all extremely helpful.
I am overwhelmed by the caring and support that I
receive, especially from fellow students/coaches and
TeleClass leaders. The executives and very seasoned
coaches also make themselves available. A great example of this is that as a student you will receive a newsletter from the President of Coach U EVERY WEEK. You
will also find that information on how to contact him is
freely available."*
– Norene Elverrillo, thrivecoach@hotmail.com

Summing Up…

As you have read, there are many advantages to enrolling in Coach U's
Coach Training Program. But key to your decision will be the people you
want to learn with. There are a number of common qualities that our participants share. See if these statements are true of you:

They are bright.
Coach U has a history of attracting the best and brightest coaches and
coaches-to-be. They have the intellectual capacity to handle the study
materials, the emotional intelligence to intuit powerfully and the personal
presence to be someone that clients want to work with.

They are eager to learn.
The individuals who choose to come into Coach U already know a lot about
people and about life. But they also know that there is more to learn about
how to coach people to be successful and happy. They are willing to make
this investment in themselves and in their professional skill set.

They understand the opportunity.
Becoming a coach is a personal, professional and business opportunity.

A personal opportunity, in the sense that you will grow and evolve yourself as you become a coach. A professional opportunity, because you develop a skill set that is universally applicable in every field of endeavor. Finally, becoming a coach is a business opportunity, since coaching is a potentially lucrative career that can allow you to design a delightful lifestyle.

They know this is the right step for themselves.
Timing is everything and the individuals who enter Coach U either know – or have decided – that this is the right time to do so. They also know that this type of investment pays off over a lifetime and attracts new people and new opportunities to them.

They are willing to be our partners.
As you have read elsewhere in this book, Coach U is a very special place. On one hand, you are our customer and we strive to keep you satisfied by sharing with you all we have. On the other hand, we are all in this together, given the emerging nature of this profession and the craft of coaching. Therefore, we need your input, collaboration and support as well. The way we see it, coaching has just begun and we are raising this baby together.

OTHER QUESTIONS ABOUT COACHING ANSWERED

Can I earn a living at this?

Yes, you can. It takes an average of between six months and four years for a coach to have enough clients to go full-time. The more people you know, the faster you can build your practice. Coach U offers dozens of classes and marketing tools on client acquisition and retention. We're not saying that building a practice is an overnight process, but thousands of coaches have done it; many of the same coaches who feared they couldn't. How much you earn depends on your marketing efforts, your area of specialty and the size and strength of your network. After several years of coaching, most coaches earn between $50,000 and $100,000. Some earn $250,000 and more.

"I took on my coach to start my coaching practice. I had two paying clients within the first week."
– Keith Collins, Keith@incondition.freeserve.com.uk, www.coachreferral.com/coaches/c/collins1001910.html

"I made $60,000 my first year of full time coaching and just went up from there. The only thing stopping me from making half a million is that I'm having too much fun doing other things. I only coach nine days a month and have been in six figures for several years."
– Jay Perry, Jay@CoachingCollective.com, www.CoachingCollective.com

Do coaches do anything other than coach clients individually?

Yes, often they do. Many offer group coaching, lead TeleClasses, conduct local workshops, do presentations, make speeches, offer audiotapes and distribute e-newsletters. Some even develop their own virtual university (like Coach U is, but with a specialty focus such as WomenU, SuccessU, ExecutiveU). The point is that you can coach as much as you wish or offer extra services to your clients locally and/or globally. Being a coach gives you a platform to offer multiple services and products, without the typical limits of most professions. That said, there's no pressure to do more than coach clients 1-1, but it's nice to know that you have so many options as you create your own professional path.

"As a Professional Organizer Coach, in addition to coaching clients individually, I also present workshops on Getting Organized and on becoming a Professional Organizer. Also, I have a professionally produced audiotape and workbook set that I offer for sale. It all works together to create a successful, exciting and diverse coaching career."
– Mary Sigmann, HarmonyPro@aol.com

"I combine coaching and more traditional consulting, about half of each. They complement and cross-pollinate each other nicely. I learn new skills and get new customers from both arenas."
– Soren Holm, soren@utveckling.nu

Where will my clients come from?

Your clients will come from your network, meaning the people that you already know and people that they know. Some people in your network will become clients and others in your network will refer clients to you. In the Coach Training Program, we show you how to expand your network tenfold, in a non-selling, non-pushy manner. You are free to advertise and promote your services in traditional ways, but we've found that this rarely works. However, we have developed a list of 101 ways to fill your practice, so you'll have an extensive menu of proven methods to select from.

"A whole new world (literally) opened up for me when I got involved with Coach U...I now feel like a citizen of the world. My clients also reflect the international exposure I get from Coach U. I now coach couples from Moscow, El Salvador, Canada, all across America and the UK. Helping people on a global basis is a great source of joy to me."
– Ed Shea, CoachIMAGO@aol.com

"By far the most effective way I have found to find clients is to teach TeleClasses on personal development subjects. In a class, the student can get an experience of what I am like – the way I see life and what I have to offer in terms of experience and perspective. This experience makes it very comfortable for a person to hire me."
– David Buck, dave@davebuck.com, www.davebuck.com

What licensing is required to be a coach?

Currently, there are virtually no requirements by any state or country that requires a coach to be licensed or approved by a governmental agency. However, in some states (in the U.S.) a coach needs to register with the state if they present themselves out as a career counselor. And, of course, coaches don't give legal, investment or psychological advice so that protects them from crossing the lines of any of the licensed professions. Students at Coach U receive up-to-the minute updates on local registration or licensing requirements. Fortunately, it is currently a non-issue for most coaches. Obviously, if you are currently licensed as a professional such as a therapist, career counselor or investment advisor, you will need to make it clear to clients when you are wearing your coaching hat.

Are there other coach training firms?

Yes, there are at least a dozen such firms, with several more forming each year. Every firm offers a particular approach to coach training and coaching. It gets a little tricky to compare ourselves with other firms, but I can say that Coach U's Coach Training Program is the only complete, comprehensive, multidisciplinary, innovative and flexible program available today. We are also the largest and only worldwide coach training firm.

> *"There are other coach training firms and I looked into all of them before joining Coach U; I am one of those people who study up on things before parting with my cash. Coach U was the only coaching firm that met and exceeded my high expectations and requirements."*
> *– Gavin Ingham, gavin@harvest.freeserve.co.uk*

> *"I researched a number of coach training programs, but when all was said and done I selected Coach U. I must say that this was an excellent choice. They provided a great combination of written materials and live training. A few days after I received my materials another much smaller package arrived from Coach U. I was surprised to find a Christmas gift in the form of a series of audiotapes on Laser Coaching. Little did I know that this was only a small expression of President Sandy Vilas' generosity. I continue to be overwhelmed by Coach U's generosity, support and willingness to do anything in their power to grow and develop me as a coach and as a person. Although I may consider also attending other training programs I will always be a part of and remain connected to Coach U."*
> *– Norene Elverrillo, thrivecoach@hotmail.com*

Can a person coach part-time?

Yes. Most coaches do, at least initially. If you already have a job, business or are freelancing, we suggest that you set aside one or two evenings a week and fit clients into a specific block of time. As you attract more clients, you'll feel more confident about making the transition to coaching 10-30 hours a week. There aren't any "shoulds" or "can'ts" in this field. Set up your coaching business in the way that suits you, your schedule and your life best.

> *"It was my intention right from the beginning to coach part-time and that is what I am doing. It fits so well into my current job of caring for my young son. The beauty of it is that I can choose to work one hour or 40 hours a week. It's all up to me."*
> *– Kathryn Andrew, mycoach@bigpond.com, www.users.bigpond.com/mycoach/*

"As a coach, your schedule is completely up to you. You can coach as much or as little as you like. Some people choose coaching as their full-time profession while others coach only a few hours per week. Coaching is like the Burger King™ approach to a career...Have it your way!"
– Dawn M. Osborn, M.S., Dawn@keys-to-success.com, www.keys-to-success.com

How long do clients stay with a coach?

The range is from three months to five years. As your coaching skills increase, clients tend to stay with you longer for two reasons. First, the client will get better results because you're doing a terrific job. Second, because as you become a stronger coach, you'll start attracting stronger, well-fitting clients, who stay with you longer.

"My clients average about one and a half years with me. The longest has been six years. Maybe that's because I want a lot for my clients. I want them to enjoy every day. In fact, the clients that stay simply enjoy our relationship. Yes, there are accomplishments and growth...that's very important. But I wouldn't be so interested in that if the process weren't so much fun."
– Jay Perry, Jay@CoachingCollective.com, www.CoachingCollective.com

"Some coaches do short-term intensive coaching for three to six months with clients around specific goals they want to achieve. Most of my clients have stayed with me for over a year because they enjoy having a mentor in their lives with whom they can discuss any personal or business issue."
– Salila Shen, heartcoach@frontier.net

"I ask a new client to consider that we will work togeth-er six months. This is not as a contract with me, rather as a commitment they make to themselves. They may re-evaluate and stop the coaching at any time. I have many clients that have stayed with me as their coach for two years. I found that it works best for both of us if we stop after two years. They may take a three month break (or more) from coaching, or start right away with another coach (I offer a referral). Either of these gives the client a fresh perspective."
– Barbara Hannah, barbara@lovinglife.net

When should I start working with clients?

As soon as you wish. The more clients you coach – even for free - the more you'll benefit from the Coach Training Program. Some coaches start coaching clients within two weeks of starting the CTP; others wait six months. It's entirely up to you. One thing that needs to be said, however, is that you do NOT need to wait until you know it all. If you meet someone who you know you can help, offer to so do and let him or her know you're new at this. Remember, every single person in this world is ALREADY a coach. The Coach Training Program simply advances your coaching skills and helps you turn your strengths into a viable coaching practice.

> *"I started working with clients right after my first month of TeleClasses at Coach U. There I heard enough coaching and other coaches to get the flavor and this validated my previous experience where I coached many people, just not calling it 'coaching.' When I was fearful about not being competent enough yet, my coach said, 'You can effectively coach SOME people right now.' He was so right! With my background and life experience, there were plenty of people who could benefit from consistent support and coaching from me. The key was for me to focus on that target market, not the prospects I wasn't ready for!"*
> *– Barbara Hannah, barbara@lovinglife.net*

> *"The key is to take clients straight away. If you really don't want to charge, then don't. The courses make more sense when you are coaching and once you start you won't want to stop!"*
> *– Gavin Ingham, gavin@harvest.freeserve.co.uk*

Can a dependency be created between coach and client?
Not really. If a client is really needy or emotionally dependent, they should be seeing a counselor, not a coach. The coach is more of a collaborative partner and works with individuals who want THAT, not help resolving emotional issues. The coach is helping the client to create a better future – more success, less stress and a more rewarding life.

> *"A coach helps a client come to his or her own decisions and realizations. A coach will not 'solve it for you.' In the end, you are the one who will take the action. Coaching is about becoming less dependent and more interdevelopmental."*
> *– Kathy Pike, kathyp@tesser.com,*
> *www.CoachKPike.com*

If I enter the Coach Training Program, what can I expect from Coach U?
You're entering a new field and we will do a number of things to support your success, including:
– Providing you with the training and information you need to coach well.

- Helping you fill your practice, to whatever extent you wish, via classes, marketing tools and advice.
- Shipping to you our complete Reference Library, which contains thousands of coaching tools.
- Connecting you with other coaches and experts in the Coach U Network.

> *"I cannot sing the praises of Coach U enough! Whatever you want, they seem to find a way of doing it. Updated methods, classes, emails, internet savvy, coaching, community – whatever you want – it's there for you!"*
> *– Gavin Ingham, gavin@harvest.freeserve.co.uk*

Okay, what do you expect of students entering Coach U?
In order for this to work, we need from you:
- A commitment to be the best possible coach, not just a good coach.
- A willingness to learn and grow, even in areas you think you know a lot already.
- A readiness to be a model for your clients, instead of just being an expert.
- A desire to be our partner in furthering the coaching profession.

Who do you recommend NOT enter Coach U?
Coach U doesn't advertise much and most of our students are referred by our current students or graduates. Usually, someone hears about Coach U, then they want more information. They either read this book, visit our website or take one of the free TeleClasses on coaching that we offer to anyone who's interested. By that time, most people are pretty sure that coaching is right for them or is not. They also know by that time whether Coach U is part of their success strategy. So, we don't have to screen heavily – the right people are naturally attracted. That said, however, we do ask people who are emotionally or financially stressed not to enter the Coach Training Program until they are ready. Learning to become a coach is an investment in a strong future, not a quick solution to current personal or professional problems. If you're not ready right now to enter the Coach Training Program, working with a coach yourself before entering may speed your preparation process and make it a lot more fun.

> *"People who think they are entering a trade school think they will gain a skill or credential by simply taking courses. In contrast, you live and breathe coaching at Coach U. You get a community of other coaches that is so thick and tenacious that you'd have to scrape them off like barnacles on submerged wood. Coach U is not for the faint of heart or for loners, but for people-people."*
> *– Meryl Moritz, urbancowgirl@worldnet.att.net*

Will I need to hire my own coach to become a coach?

This is entirely up to you. The most successful coaches (those making $75,000-$250,000 year) hired a mentor coach in order to ramp up more quickly and continually evolve themselves. Currently, about 50% of the coaches-in-training at Coach U work with what are called Mentor Coaches. Fees range from $100 (group coaching) to $400 (1-1 coaching) a month.

> *"I can't image not having a coach myself as I coach others. To be able to be my very best, it is so helpful to have someone who understands what might interfere with my being the best coach ever. Since I finally found the perfect occupation for me, why mess around with it?"*
> *– Jo Ann Heiser, lifecoachjo@juno.com*

> *"When I first enrolled in Coach U, I knew I wanted to become a professional coach. I had no intention of hiring a coach for myself because I figured I could get all I needed through the courses. Although it is not mandatory to have a coach, I cannot imagine trying to be a coach without ever having been coached! After several months in Coach U it became obvious: the best coaches have or have had their own coaches."*
> *– Renee Lanman, ReneeLan@aol.com*

Are coaches specializing?
If so, what are the most popular specialties?

Yes, they are. There are at least 100 specialties a coach can focus on. These are listed in the Appendix.

> *"I have chosen to conduct a practice that puts coaching in a Christian framework and I find that works very well. Some clients come to me for spiritual direction but I prefer to call it 'spiritual and personal coaching' as it seems impossible to isolate an area of your life in that way and do truly effective work."*
> *– Kathryn Andrew, mycoach@bigpond.com,*
> *www.users.bigpond.com/mycoach/*

What kind of background does a person need to have in order to be an effective coach?

We are asked this question a lot. Educationally, it's nice to have a degree (over 90% of our students do), but that's not required. There are many bright and effective coaches working without a college degree. Socially, coaches come from every background, given coaching is trans-cultural and cross-cultural. You don't need to be an expert in everything, but you should have a personal spark, some life experience and a huge willingness to learn the craft of coaching. Your clients want YOU as their coach; they don't want a coaching service. Use the training at Coach U to improve the YOU of you and increase your professional skill set.

"It isn't about background. A person from any background can become a coach. It is more about the nature of who you are and what would give meaning to your life. Are you naturally drawn to excellence? Helping people? Caring? Authenticity? There are people with these qualities from every background. You don't even have to have any skill to get started, just willingness and the courage to try."
– Maggie Hanna, Mjhanna@telusplanet.net

"I have found that people come from many different backgrounds to be effective coaches. My background consists of degrees in psychology and educational psychology and 16 years as a stay-at-home mom living overseas. This has helped me to be especially effective with moms in transition and ex-pats. Other coaches I know come from financial, business, therapy, theatrical and marketing backgrounds. They each have a special blend of talents to work with any client as well as specialized talents and experience. To me this is what makes coaching so special. If you want to, you can find a coach with life experiences similar to yours and have instant rapport."
– Gail Valenti, lgvalenti@aol.com

What do you look for in a coach to know if they will be successful?
There are two different types of success.

One type of success is measured by how effective a coach is with their clients: How quickly does the client reach their goals? How easily? How much does the client grow and evolve? How well does the coach bring out the client's best? For this measure of success, the primary thing we look for is the prospective coach's willingness – and eagerness – to learn. To learn coaching skills, strategies, phrasing, the coaching technology. Coaching is not for dilettantes looking for the next diversion – coaching is a profession and a broad skill set and learning is key to mastering it.

The other type of success in coaching is measured by how successful the coach's practice is. How many clients do they have? How easy is it for them to attract clients? Are they making enough money? The coaches who become the most financially successful are the coaches who are willing to give their clients exactly what the client wants and needs. In other words, these coaches respond to the marketplace instead of limiting themselves to one way of thinking or a single specialty. So, flexibility and a desire to serve on the client's terms are key to a coach's financial success.

What is Coach U's history?

I first started training coaches in 1988, with a group of 12 coaches. One of those coaches was Sandy Vilas, who became the owner of Coach U in 1996. (I am now the Director of R&D.) Coach U officially started in

1992 with 100 coaches starting the Coach Training Program. Since then over 3,800 coaches have entered the Training Program. Based on current trends we expect over 2,000 coaches to start their training at Coach U in 2000. We have the infrastructure and trainers to handle about 10,000 coaches at one time, so we're prepared. Over the years, we've added dozens of client programs that coaches can use with clients, produced 500 hours of audiotapes, 4000 pages of reference materials, coined such terms at Clean Sweep, Personal Foundation, The Attraction Approach, Personal Evolution, TeleClass and Certified Coach, among others. The secret of our success is the partnership we have developed with students and graduates alike. We help them; they help us. We are all on a single mission here and that is to train the finest coaches in the world.

Coaching and Coach U certainly have received a lot of media attention in the past several years. Why is that?

The emergence of an important new profession IS newsworthy. So newsworthy in fact that over 250 media stories have appeared on coaching and Coach U since 1996. When Newsweek magazine did a full-page article on coaching and Coach U, that opened the doors to coverage by USA Today, Donahue, the New York Times, the Times of London, CBS This Morning, NBC Nightly News, CNN's Impact, Inc., New Age Journal and scores of metropolitan daily newspapers and news programs around the world. Thanks to the media's coverage, most people know what coaching is and don't ask if you coach Little League when you say you are a professional coach. We've come a long way from the earliest days when half of the conversation was just to explain what coaching is.

> *"The public is very interested in coaching at the moment and it is the perfect time to get into coaching. But coaching is no fad! Coaching works and the media knows it. Coach U gets attention because they get results!"*
> *– Gavin Ingham, gavin@harvest.freeserve.co.uk*

Do you ever hear from people who say that coaching sounds like the perfect profession for them and that they wish they had heard about Coach U earlier?

Yes, we hear this all the time. Coach U doesn't advertise and we rely on word of mouth and media coverage to get the word out, so we apologize if we didn't make ourselves known earlier. But not to worry! Coaching is still in its infancy and is just getting started, so you're coming in at a perfect time.

> *"I was working as a consultant to small businesses. Following a consulting session I had with a close friend, we were discussing some personal things and I expressed that I was more interested in having my own business than consulting to others. When she asked me to describe my ideal profession I described to the*

letter what I later learned was coaching. Two days later by a miracle I discovered coaching as a profession. I had actually been coaching all my life but only recently learned that I could make a living through this work."
– Norene Elverrillo, thrivecoach@hotmail.com

"Coaching with Coach U has provided a context to draw together all my training, consulting and facilitating experience into one flexible, comprehensive, dynamic and credible system. My only regret is I did not discover it sooner."
– Wendy Buckingham, classone@zeta.org.au

"Coaching is the definitive profession for me. I have been studying for coaching for the last 10 years - I just never called it that. When I first read about coaching in the Sunday Times, it seemed to be exactly what I had been looking for."
– Gavin Ingham, gavin@harvest.freeserve.co.uk

Does coaching conflict with religious, spiritual or cultural beliefs?

Coaching itself doesn't present a conflict with most people, but some of the Success Principles and concepts discussed at Coach U may be different than you've learned or in which you believe. Our job is to expand every student's way of thinking to be as inclusive as possible. We want you to see all of the options available to a client. We are not asking you to change your beliefs or use ours – we want you to be YOU, not us. But we do ask that you at least be willing to learn additional ways of coaching and advising. Every coach is unique and people come to Coach U in order to learn from each other.

"I have always been a deeply spiritual person and have extensive training in both Eastern and Western spiritual traditions. At Coach U I discovered that though spirit is seldom mentioned and no particular tradition is advanced, the people drawn to Coach U are deeply spiritual and I feel completely at home and supported in my own spirituality though I seldom need to make reference to it. What a blessing."
– Michael Sheffield, mscoach@sonic.net

"As a Christian minister, I have been able to incorporate a great deal of the Coach U materials into my coaching practice. Sometimes it requires that I change my perspective slightly or explain something a little differently, but generally I have found little that I think others would take offense at. Remember, it's what you choose to make it. You don't have to agree with it all! I just take on board the things I feel are suitable for my clients and

fit my own spiritual and religious paradigms. Coaching is a way of getting the most out of the life God gave you, not a strict code of ideas or set behaviors. You'll do well to remember this if you have fundamentalist tendencies!"
– Kathryn Andrew, mycoach@bigpond.com, www.users.bigpond.com/mycoach/

Why has coaching become so popular?

Coaching has become so popular (20,000 coaches worldwide at last guestimate) because there is a consumer demand for it. Few coaches advertise or market heavily so most clients come via referral, which is an excellent filter. There are many reasons that coaching has become so popular. First, as more individuals become self-employed or start their own business, they want the structure, support and wisdom to help them be a success, given the potentially steep learning curve. Second, people are becoming more creative, selfish (in a good sense) and excited about life. People want to do more, be more, get more and a coach is seen as a partner in this process. Third, time has become even more valuable and people don't want to wait for ANYTHING anymore. A coach can usually help a client get what they want FASTER.

"Coaching is for the millenium and beyond. With a job for life no longer existing, the current economic climate, downsizing and job-sharing people need a stronger base in life. Coaching helps people realize what is important in their lives and supports them in honoring those values. Family, personal integrity, generosity...these are the buzzwords for the next millennium and coaching is the perfect solution for clients seeking to truly live their own values."
– Gavin Ingham, gavin@harvest.freeserve.co.uk

Does a person become a coach for a lifetime?

They can if they want. After several years in this field, you can pretty much pick your clients and set your own course. Some coaches will coach for the next 30 years and absolutely love it. Others will coach for five years and then select another career – one that probably uses many of the skills and principles they learned and used as a coach. Others will stay in their current job or profession and simply weave in the coaching technology. Your path will be entirely up to you, and you likely will learn the next phase of your path when it comes upon you, rather than planning it years in advance.

"From my experience in the Coach U community, I feel most coaches would say that they didn't 'become' a coach, but have been coaching their whole lives (for free!) without realizing there was a name for what they were doing. Once I discovered that there was a newly-

emerging profession called 'coaching,' I knew I had
found a way to offer my gifts through my work."
– Salila Shen, heartcoach@frontier.net

"If you are drawn to be a coach, most likely you are
already. Coach U will help you develop and refine your
skills to be the best coach you can be. Once you real-
ize the gift you have to share, you most likely will do so
for the rest of your life. It may take form in another
way, but the basic premise of providing space and
opportunity for different perspectives and action will
remain."
– Kathy Pike, kathyp@tesser.com,
www.CoachKPike.com

Summing Up...

Coaching is an emerging and exciting field, drawing to it many of the best
and brightest from a number of other fields. The results coaches' clients
produce speak for themselves and are causing the profession to grow more
than heavy marketing ever could. We're happy to answer any question you
have about the industry we pioneered and continue to develop. Call us at
1-800-48COACH, 24 hours day. Or, email us at help@coachu.com.

SECTION 11

OTHER QUESTIONS ABOUT THE COACH TRAINING PROGRAM ANSWERED

Can I speak with students and graduates of the program?

Yes. The best way is to go to the Coach Referral website and search for coaches in your area or in your field of interest. Coaches' email addresses and phone numbers are included in their listings and most welcome calls from individuals such as yourself who are curious about coaching and Coach U. It is very likely that they, too, reached out to speak with students and graduates, when they were considering entering Coach U. Just go to http://www.coachreferral.com. Another option is that the coaches who have shared their comments with us in this book are also available via email to answer your questions. Feel free to write any of them.

> *"I spoke with five different students and graduates of Coach U between the first time I called to inquire about the program and the day I enrolled. Each person was willing to share their own personal experience with Coach U, coaching in general and answer any questions I had. Yet, no one ever applied pressure to enroll and they always made clear that it is a personal choice to be made from one's own timetable. The personal interaction with the people involved was a major factor in my decision."*
> – Marilyn Hall, halls@intur.net

> *"When I was researching my coach-training options, I had the opportunity to speak with more than ten different coaches from across the country. Each coach had a growing, dynamic practice thanks to Coach U's training and preparation. The coaches I spoke with described how they developed successful practices while still completing classes at Coach U. The unique training approach Coach U offers incorporates the concept that training is not just gathering knowledge, but rather it involves putting knowledge into practice. By coaching clients while at Coach U, we have the opportunity to demonstrate real learning by putting knowledge into practice."*
> – Jane Yousey, ReachnHigh@aol.com

Do coaches from Coach U ever meet together in person?

Yes, they do. Coach U offers periodic live trainings in the U.S. and major cities worldwide. And the 100+ Coach U Chapters meet monthly. For a list of cities, please see the Appendix. For a list of upcoming trainings and chapter meetings, go to the Coach U website at http://www.coachu.com. These chapter meetings are open to the public, so you are most welcome to attend and meet coaches in your area. They

81

are happy to welcome you and to answer your questions about coaching, coach training and our profession. Most meetings are informal and include a group discussion on a current theme or coaching topic. Chapter meetings are not selling events. They are meetings with coaches and coaches-to-be. Your chapter host can tell you more.

Coach U also sponsors an annual training conference in the summer that brings together coaches from around the world.

Do I have to have a computer or be on the Internet in order to enter the CTP?

Yes. If you don't have a computer now but are planning to buy one within 30 days, you may still enter the CTP. We can even provide system recommendations if you like. You may select a Windows or Macintosh computer system. Our system is cross-platform. If you already have a computer and aren't yet on the Internet, we can help you there as well. Our customer service department can get you started and even make ISP recommendations (an ISP is the company that provides you access to the Internet, like AOL, Earthlink, etc.). And we offer several CyberSkills classes to coaches at no additional charge on everything from e-mail, surfing the web and creating your own website. Many coaches start Coach U with little computer experience, but our supportive staff and TeleClass leaders get them up and running in no time. In the Appendix, you'll see the titles of these course in the TeleClass area.

> "When I first started with Coach U I was using my sister's computer. It became evident in the first two weeks that I needed my own. I did not 'get' how much information was available to me through the Coach U website and other coachs' websites. I also did not comprehend the amount of communication that occurs through e-mail. I have many virtual friends that I will look forward to meeting at my first Coaching conference. I have discovered that I enjoy the technology of the Internet and I am currently developing my own web page. I recommend having a computer and getting online before you start your classes. Coach U also provides classes on how to be more efficient online!"
> – Kathy Pike, kathyp@tesser.com,
> www.CoachKPike.com

Why do I have to be on the Internet in order to enter the CTP?

Several reasons. One is that you register for TeleClasses via our 24-hour a day, automated web-based system. You also receive updates and special invitations and news via e-mail. You can also view the newly added materials with your web browser and even use our growing collection of interactive tools. Also, most of your clients will be on the Internet, so you'll need to be there, as well. If you've been putting it off, here's your chance to be supported through the process of getting connected. Within 60 days of being online, you'll recognize how essential it is to your professional and financial success.

"With the internet we can communicate with coaches from around the world. It is so exciting to exchange thoughts and ideas with people you may otherwise never have an opportunity to meet. The Internet also allows you to access Coach U's information at any time. I'm not restricted by my personal schedule or awkward time zones!"
– Kim Johnson, kimkj6@earthlink.net, www.nursewatch.com

"The Coach U TeleClass program is rich and powerful and will train you how to be an excellent coach. But if you want to experience the richness of the community Coach U has to offer, you must get on the Internet. It is in the e-mail and casual interaction between students, Special Interest Group (SIG) participants and the weekly Coach U newsletters that this richness lives. Without it, you will only be getting half the experience of Coach U."
– Rinatta Paries, Coach@WhatItTakes.com, www.WhatItTakes.com

I am already trained in some of the subjects you teach; do I have to take the entire program?

To graduate you'll need to take at least 200 units (hours) of training via TeleClasses. You will be required to take the core modules (160 hours worth), but you may select your other 40 hours worth from a wide collection of available electives. So, even if you are already a therapist, counselor, consultant or trainer, you will be amazed at how sophisticated the coaching process is. You will quickly recognize how distinct and extensive the coaching skill set and coaching approach is, even if you've mastered the skills in your own field. Even if you don't plan to offer business coaching, you will find the business-oriented modules extremely helpful, given the coming convergence of work and play in the next decade. You need to know how both work.

"There are certainly aspects of the Coach U program that I covered in my training to become an ordained minister. But what I discovered when I entered the program was that despite this, each module made me hungry for more and more and more! And I soon discovered that because the learning is done via TeleClass, that even though the subject matter may overlap with past learning, the unique perspective that each group of students brings to the class means you are never really doing the same thing twice. I would recommend to anyone, regardless of their background, that they invest in doing the complete program. We never stop learning!"
– Kathryn Andrew, mycoach@bigpond.com, www.users.bigpond.com/mycoach/

"You can take the classes you want and/or need at your own discretion (and as many times as you want). I would recommend, however, that you attend all the classes because there is ALWAYS something to learn from these sessions. The other students/coaches come from various backgrounds and experiences and what they have to offer is very rich. Once you participate in the classes you will find that the generosity is contagious and you will want to attend classes in areas that you are already trained in so that you can share your experience for the benefit of others."
– Norene Elverrillo, thrivecoach@hotmail.com

Can I hire a Mentor Coach instead of entering the Coach Training Program?

I suppose so, but you'd miss the point. A Mentor Coach is trained to help you make the most of the Coach Training Program, not to actually be your personal training program. Only via Coach U can you learn (and be permitted to use) the hundreds of coaching skills, proprietary programs and marketing tools. Your Mentor Coach is for you, but doesn't train you in the Coach U technology.

"You should do both! You will find that the community at Coach U will mentor you along with your coach! It is a very rich experience to be coached during class by many others with varying backgrounds, experiences and styles. The training and having a coach definitely complement each other. I would not want to be without either one while beginning a career as a coach."
– Norene Elverrillo, thrivecoach@hotmail.com

"Sure you could hire a mentor instead of entering the Coach Training Program, but it would be like being fed instead of learning to fish."
– Maggie Hanna, Mjhanna@telusplanet.net

"The tools needed to evolve into a successful coach are like those needed to build a house – you can't just use a hammer or just a screwdriver. Rather, the Coach Training Program provides a vast library of coaching material, an online resource of additional tools, an expansive network of coaches from around the world who provide mentoring support, a broad online referral network, newsletters, etc., which all combine to fill the coach's toolbox with everything he/she needs to develop into a successful coach."
– Jane Yousey, ReachnHigh@aol.com

How do I know I am getting my tuition's worth?

The tuition works out to about $5 a day for the two years of the program (the average time it takes students to graduate), so it's very difficult to imagine that you wouldn't get your money's worth by entering the program. The last thing we ever want to do is to push someone to enter Coach U. Again, you either love the idea of becoming a coach or you don't. We've built in over $10,000 of value into the Coach Training Program, yet priced it to make it available for as many people as possible who wish to be a coach. Remember, too, once you graduate, you can come back for more classes at no additional charge. And you always receive the updated materials and program and access to the RealAudio tape collection at no additional charge.

"I realized I had received my value from the Coach U tuition when my first client told me the profound difference I had made in their life and how appreciative they were. That awareness of value returns to me each time I realize how much my own life has changed. Other coaches have shared this same sense with me: Maybe you feel freer, or you are filled with more joy, or your friends are new and different, or your finances are better, or you feel better about who you are and what you have to share. One day you realize that the quality of your life has changed drastically and you can have fun helping others create this life for themselves. I love it!"
– Kathy Pike, kathyp@tesser.com,
www.CoachKPike.com

"I have been connecting with and guiding people all my life, but coaching has given me the tools to reach and touch others in a whole new way. Since joining Coach U, I realize that my own personal growth and development have far exceeded my wildest dreams. If I never had a client, the Coach U training would have been worth every penny and every minute just for ME! But I do have clients...many...and I'm good at what I do. I now have the means to help others propel themselves and we both enjoy every moment of the process."
– Judy Irving, Uramiracle@aol.com

"I know I have got my money's worth from Coach U. The materials are fabulous and the fact that you can reproduce the client forms is such a bonus. Everything you need to know is provided in the printed materials you receive or get on-line. And where else can you learn from such professionals in the comfort of your armchair? My Coach U fee has provided me with my own personal gold mine for a lifetime!"
– Kathryn Andrew, mycoach@bigpond.com,
www.users.bigpond.com/mycoach/

"Going to Coach U is worth every dime even if you never become a coach. Who wouldn't invest money into a program that restores you to a life of prosperity and peace?"
– Lyn Christian, coachlyn@hotmail.com

Why don't you charge for annual upgrades or post-graduate training?

We never have and don't plan to. Why not? Several reasons: First, the more graduates feel like they can stick around and benefit from the newly developed work, the better coaches they will be and this makes us look even better! Second, the graduates are the veteran coaches and we love having them evolve into partners with us – it is in everyone's best interest to keep them happy and engaged. Finally, we can afford to offer post-graduate training at no charge because of the many volunteers who help to defray our operating expenses.

"Making the upgrades and post-graduate training free of charge is one way that Coach U demonstrates their continued commitment to grow you as a coach and person. It is also in line with their spirit of generosity and support. It's really great to be supported by an organization of this quality."
– Norene Elverrillo, thrivecoach@hotmail.com

Are there other costs in the Coach Training Program?

The tuition covers all 200+ hours of TeleClasses, lifetime web access, responsive customer service, the printed complete Reference Library with free electronic upgrades, lifetime listing in the CoachReferral.com site, RealAudio versions of classes/tapes, free training in TeleClass Leading and licensing of our client programs such as Personal Foundation and Attraction (with some exceptions for group delivery on some programs). Tuition does not cover the costs of hiring your own mentor coach (optional) or your long distance call to our conferencing bridges (located in San Francisco, Las Vegas and Orlando). There are no other charges.

"Since paying my Coach U tuition, I have not spent another dime at their request. The price that I paid has bought me extensive materials, updates, an incredibly supportive community, new tools as they are developed, opportunities to participate in so many different things, the latest information and developments in the profession, added value each year, including new classes and much, much, more! I will say it again: all this at no additional cost to me. I have only spent money on telephone calls (which Coach U has helped with by providing access to a long distance service with great rates), purchasing books (that I wanted for my own benefit) and setting up a web page. I also

invested in hiring a coach of my own."
– Norene Elverrillo, thrivecoach@hotmail.com

Don't the phone calls get expensive?

Long distance costs continue to drop. Some services offer long distance as low as 5 or 9 cents a minute, 24 hours a day. But for now, figure about $5 per one-hour session; by the end of the year 2000, expect it to be as low as $1 per hour. You may use any long distance carrier you wish and there are no special conference call charges given that our teleconference bridge system is fully automated and that we lease it. We're all the more pleased when coaches make the effort to call in for live classes from Europe, Japan, the UK and other regions of the world. Coaching is a worldwide phenomenon.

> *"I have made all my TeleClass calls from my home in Perth, in Western Australia...the most isolated city in the world! It took a little while in the beginning to sort out phone plans and service providers but I have managed to cut my bill to 2/3 of the original cost by some research. Now it costs no more to do a TeleClass than it would cost to pay for petrol and parking going to a university! It seems like your phone bill is going to be enormous but it doesn't really wash with reality. If money is really tight, just do one class at a time."*
> *– Kathryn Andrew, mycoach@bigpond.com, www.users.bigpond.com/mycoach/*

> *"Calling from Sweden they do get expensive. But after a time I had enough paying clients to easily cover the cost and then some."*
> *– Soren Holm, soren@utveckling.nu*

What happens during a typical TeleClass?

Most of the formal training you receive in the Coach Training Program is done via conference call. Class members all call into one of our teleconferencing bridges for an hour at a time and work their way through one of the modules of the program. Each of the 36 core classes consists of at least four weeks of training, so registered students meet at the same time each week for four weeks. Most TeleClasses are 55 minutes in length and are conveniently scheduled throughout the day – in the morning, afternoon and evening. Each session is conducted by a Coach U Trainer. The format is interactive, much like a graduate-school discussion. The trainer covers the key points of the module and works with students to understand, integrate and learn the coaching concepts, skills or strategies of that module. Students also engage in role-plays, peer coaching and case studies, depending on the module. The TeleClasses are a highly experiential system of learning, and they are a lot of fun. Training doesn't have to be boring. After all, life is not boring!

"Coach U prides itself in producing programs that are incredibly fun and that stretch you. The TeleClasses are not effortless but they are extraordinarily rewarding. They will provide you with opportunities to grow and expand like you've rarely, if ever, experienced before. And most importantly, Coach U TeleClasses produce results!"
– David Shockley, David@Nextstepcoaching.com, www.Nextstepcoaching.com

"During the hour-long session, coaches have the opportunity not only to gain knowledge and hear about new skills as course curriculum is discussed, but also to participate in a real-time coaching experience, thus shifting from knowledge to real learning. Class participants role-play the client/coach relationship, often with real situations the student coach or one of her clients is facing, while the class leader mentors throughout the class. The uniqueness of TeleClasses revolves around the people who are in them. Each participant contributes gems of insight and experience, so that TeleClass learning offers a richness far greater than a traditional classroom model of learning could offer."
– Jane Yousey, ReachnHigh@aol.com

"Initially, I was hesitant to enroll at Coach U because of the format. I am very much a people person and felt that I would miss a lot by dealing via telephone. I had also planned to coach my clients in person. I spoke with Alison Hendren (Director of Admissions at Coach U) who was returning my call from Canada and the quality of the conversation eliminated any doubts I had about the effectiveness of learning and coaching by phone. Once enrolled in the classes, what I had learned during the conversation was confirmed. I found the format to be very rich; participants are very attentive and even though you can't see them, their personalities and expressions come across very well by telephone. I can almost 'see' my classmates! Needless to say, I also chose to use this format with my clients and it has been very effective. It is very convenient for them and they seem to be more relaxed and open. In addition, the resources Coach U makes available to its students are incredible."
– Norene Elverrillo, thrivecoach@hotmail.com

How do I actually learn via a TeleClass? How much homework should I expect?
     You learn coaching skills, techniques and strategies in MANY ways - via TeleClasses, self-study, audiotapes, Real Audio, web-based learning, the

Reference Library and coaching of clients. But on your TeleClasses, you learn by listening, discussing and even role-playing, guided by your instructor who is an experienced coach him/herself. Most coaches in training naturally and quickly attract at least several clients and by having these clients, you use the TeleClasses as your just-in-time learning system. There is ample time for you to ask the instructor – and your colleagues on the call – how to handle a client situation or what to do more effectively. You can expect about 20 minutes of homework for every hour of TeleClass and it will vary by instructor and by class.

Who are the trainers at Coach U? What are their backgrounds?
The trainers are full-time coaches themselves. Most trainers train about 10 hours a month for Coach U, so you will be learning from real coaches, coaching real clients every day. The trainers' backgrounds are similar to the backgrounds of most coaches at Coach U – professionals, degreed, experienced, personally evolved and excited to share what they know that works with clients. Some of our trainers are specialists, meaning that they work mainly with a single type of client, such as the executive or those in career transition. Others are experts in people and understand what motivates, inspires, influences and develops people. Still others are professional strategists, who tend to teach the classes we offer that have to do with developing creating strategies for challenging client situations.

How does one become a trainer for Coach U?
Every coach at Coach U has the option to train to be a trainer at Coach U. Once you've completed at least 3/4 the required TeleClasses, you are eligible to enter the free eight week class called the TeleClass Leader Training Program, held several times a year. In this Program, you learn the fundamentals of conducting interactive/evocative TeleClasses and how to make your point in clever ways so students can learn effectively over the telephone. By the end of the 8-week training, you and we will know if you're right for leading and if you are accepted for the TeleClass Leader Training Program, you'll receive additional training and mentoring at no cost to you. Alternatively, if you are already an expert in a business or personal related area and would like to offer a TeleClass to other coaches at Coach U, you may be able to bypass this training requirement if your subject matter is mostly technical in nature and you are mostly teaching information vs. training coaches.

I live outside North America. How is the program geared toward me?
Currently, there are students and graduates from Coach U from 36 countries. Most students are English-speaking, given the original library was written in English, but already the entire library and program is available in Japanese and parts of the library are now available in French and German. Spanish, Chinese and Portuguese are next. And, as you know, it's not just the words that need translation – the cultural meanings and nuances are also a part of the process. The translations to date have been done by Coach U graduates and we are eager to work with you on translating some

or all of the materials into your language. Also, given we offer the entire training program by RealAudio as well, it would be possible to audiotape 200 hours of segments with a native speaker in your language. As you can see, the possibilities are boundless.

> *"In the UK there are huge choices of times for courses and a thriving community of coaches. Although the bulk of the activity of Coach U is in the US our message to the UK is – coaching is here!"*
> *– Gavin Ingham, gavin@harvest.freeserve.co.uk*

> *"I think an important point about becoming a CTPer and living in another country other than the U.S. is getting in early in an expanding field. Sure we want to do good in the world, but while being first with something new means more work (such as translating materials) it is also a great business advantage."*
> *– Soren Holm, soren@utveckling.nu*

Is there a Certification available?

Yes. Coach U owns the trademark Certified Coach and awards the Certified Coach designation, the most widely-respected coach certification available. Graduates from the Coach Training Program may apply for certification after having coached a minimum of 1000 hours and passing oral and written exams, among other qualifications. Currently, there are at least 10 designations offered in the coaching world, but none carry the cachet of Certified Coach because none require the depth and breadth of training and competency demanded by the Certified Coach designation. And, as much as we are proud of this designation, it should be noted that it is your ability to coach clients effectively that matters most, not a designation. Let your current clients establish your credibility instead of trying to create credibility with a designation that is not yet widely-known by the public.

What is the philosophical basis for the Coach U approach to coaching?

That's a tricky question because we are a synthesis of at least a dozen disciplines and fields of study, including organizational development, entrepreneurism, personal development, psychology, sports, the healing arts, transformation, spirituality, philosophy and marketing. In other words, we use and teach concepts, strategies, principles, theories, practices, systems, models and language from all of these fields. We weave all of these together carefully in order to produce the integrated coaching technology vs. just an amalgamated assortment of ideas. All we can say is that coaching has proven itself to work, with over 100,000 satisfied clients of Coach U-trained coaches, in the past five years. Not bad for a new profession!

Summing Up...

Coach U trains the finest coaches in the world, and we love to answer questions about our training program. Is there a question that wasn't answered here? Please call us at 1-800-48COACH, 24 hours day and we'll do our best to answer it. Or, email us at help@coachu.com. Every question is welcome; no question is unanswerable.

SECTION 12

OTHER QUESTIONS ABOUT COACH U ANSWERED

What is the Coach U Philosophy?
Our views on coaching, on people and on life are quite simple...

On coaching
We believe that our job as coaches is to help our clients get what they most want in life, personally and professionally. Everything a coach does with or for a client is oriented around that. There are no other agendas. We push for nothing but the client's true desires. And there is nothing more important than our client's satisfaction with our work.

On people
We believe that each person is unique and special in many ways and that we are all connected. We feel that as we strengthen ourselves, we strengthen everyone around us. We also feel that people are evolving, not just changing. In other words, what it means to be a person continues to evolve and unfold.

On life
We believe that life comes to us as a series of messages. If you see the message and respond to it, the message becomes an opportunity. If you ignore or don't see the message, the message becomes a problem. The better you can see and the faster you respond, the more opportunities and fewer problems you will have.

> *"The Coach U Philosophy is in complete alignment with the spiritual principles that make my life work. Integrity, generosity, service and community are at its core."*
> *– Mary Sigmann, HarmonyPro@aol.com*

What is the culture like at Coach U?
Coach U is a very special place. We are a graduate-level school. We host a worldwide network of coaches. We are a dynamic research and development facility. We are a publisher and an electronic broadcast company. And we are a professional home to over 3,800 coaches. There is no other organization like Coach U anywhere in the world.

Our vision is that everyone has a coach. Our mission is to train the finest personal and business coaches worldwide. And our purpose is to develop the most extensive collection of tools that each coach can use for the success of their clients and of their own practice.

Each individual who comes into Coach U does so in order to learn how to become an effective and successful coach in the most current, practical and comprehensive manner. Most of them are well educated and already successful in a previous career. They are adult learners and want to be stretched. They are already motivated and know what they want.

In other words, they – you – are the perfect partners for us. We share with you what we know that works with clients and you share with us what you know about life, as well as telling us what other tools and support you want us to provide. We give you the tools you need to be a successful coach and you help us to create even better tools. We do our part to help you build and maintain your practice and you help us to keep Coach U successful.

It's a mutually beneficial, inter-developmental and cooperative relationship. It's a true partnership. And it's especially helpful during this stage of the development of the coaching profession, given how much remains to be discovered and developed in order to benefit the current and future generations of coaches.

You – and we – are the kernels of an emerging profession that is growing quickly and in exciting new directions. We guide, enjoy and inspire each other.

> *"There is a culture in Coach U that encourages us all to be pioneers in the discovery of knowledge that continuously supports us all to set new standards for service excellence and product innovation. This is a community that thrives on promoting each of us to be the best coach and person, possible!"*
> *– Brenda Thibault, brenda.thibault@wd.gc.ca*

> *"'Shift happens.' That is what I discovered about myself when I entered the virtual doors of Coach U. My health, finances and daily experience of fulfillment took a giant leap forward. I am grateful to this infinitely creative and supportive group of coaches for helping me live my dream. This is the gift I give to my clients."*
> *– Michael Johnson, pathfind@vgernet.net, www.berkshirecoach.com*

> *"I have been astounded with the positive and energetic impact that Coach U has made on my life. I originally joined this organization to update skills and help with a transition in professions. Not only did I learn a completely different approach to business, but after courses such as Personal Foundation and Personal/Spiritual Path, my outlook on my own personal path shifted dramatically. I am (happily) selling a huge home, moving to another location and have opened very rewarding communication channels with the people I love most in my life."*
> *– Sharon Hooper, wolfie@interisland.net*

What is Coach U's mission?

Our mission is to train the finest coaches in the world. We fulfill this mission by offering the most comprehensive, most developed, most effective coach training program available worldwide. We continually update the content of our classes, reference materials and client programs to reflect the most recent advances made in our field. We work closely with our students in order to ensure a consistent, effective and inspiring training program.

And we work closely with our alumni to increase the breadth of the Coach Training Program so that we train coaches in the rapidly emerging specialties in the coaching profession.

When did Coach U first pioneer its programs?
Here is a very brief list of the intellectual property developed and/or milestones reached in each year of our history.

History (and Future) of Coach U
- 1988: Clean Sweep Program developed/12 coaches trained
- 1989: TeleClass format developed/10 classes a week
- 1990: Coaching Forms Book & Manual/First media coverage
- 1991: Coach Training Workshop offered/50 coaches trained
- 1992: Coach U formed/100 coaches trained in first year
- 1993: Personal Foundation Program developed/300 coaches
- 1994: The Coach U Website launched/500 coaches
- 1995: Certified Coach Designation developed/750 coaches
- 1996: Attraction Program designed/150+ positive media stories
- 1997: Corporate Coach U lauched/1,400 coaches
- 1998: Personal Evolution Program/2,500 coaches
- 1999: Coach U Conference 99/Coaching Road Tour 99
- 2000: Specialty Coach Certifications/4,000 coaches
- 2001: Coach U Training in 5 languages/10,000 coaches
- 2002: 15,000th coach trained

"I was there at the beginning. At first there was one class and one teacher. We were all so close. I was afraid that as it grew all of that would be lost. But somehow it's managed to maintain a small town kind of feel. I know I can call Sandy Vilas any time... and usually he picks up the phone. He even calls me on my birthday."
– Jay Perry, Jay@CoachingCollective.com, www.CoachingCollective.com

What are Coach U's systems and structures?
Given Coach U is a virtual organization, the delivery and customer service systems and state-of-the-art technologies we use are especially important. Briefly:

- We own 45 teleconference bridges with a weekly capacity of 100,000 students.
- Most of our TeleClasses, training programs and audiotapes (500+ hours) are available via RealAudio to our students and graduates.
- The student-only website contains 10,000 individual documents.
- We host websites for students and our related organizations.
- CoachReferral.com receives 20,000 visitors annually; over 1900 listings.
- Over 200 autoresponders give students immediate access to the most popular tools and information.

- Students register for TeleClasses in real-time, via our website, with immediate confirmations.
- The entire Coach U Library is viewable online (students only).
- 30+ staff and 80+ trainers deliver the training and operate the organization.
- We broadcast 25,000 tips, top ten lists, and newsletters each week.
- 250 volunteers develop the intellectual property, host Special Interest Groups, run the Coach U chapters worldwide and provide direction to the organization.
- Staff receive 250,000 e-mails a year.

> *"The Coach U systems of administration are designed to make your experience with them easy and trouble free. There are autoresponders to answer almost any question you might have. The website is rich in content that will both enhance your experience as a student and as a coach, and the registration system is created to allow for maximum flexibility and ease."*
> *– Rinatta Paries, Coach@WhatItTakes.com, www.WhatItTakes.com*

Summing Up...

One of the most interesting things about Coach U is how we run the business, especially given the virtual nature of it. Many students learn our business model while being trained here and then launch their own specialized virtual business (in a field other than coach training, of course).

SECTION 13

TAKING ACTION

If you're ready to begin your coach training, please complete the CTP Registration worksheet and have it ready when you speak to our admissions officer. If you would first like more information, we suggest you participate in one or more of these TeleClasses or live trainings.

1. Getting an Experience of Coach U
About 5000 people like yourself attend one or more of the following classes each year in order to get a feel for Coach U and hear answers to their specific questions about the program and training methods. It's also a great way to experience the TeleClass format firsthand if this is a new way of learning for you.

A. Coaching Q&A TeleClass - One one-hour session
A one-hour call hosted by Sandy Vilas, Coach U CEO. Sandy starts the call out with a brief overview of Coach U, the Coach Training Program and the coaching process. Feel free to ask your questions, which Sandy will answer. Every question leads to more questions and this session is very informative and a lot of fun. For these Q&A Sessions, please call 1-407-649-9054 at class time from any phone. You will be automatically connected. (Tips: Disable call waiting before calling; don't call early [no one will be there]; if you are late, please listen silently.)

For dates for classes, please call 1-800-48COACH or go to www.coachu.com.

B. 1, 2, 3, Coach! TeleClass - Four one-hour sessions
Since 1992, over 5,000 individuals have learned coaching basics from this free, four-session TeleClass. During the course, you'll learn about the coaching model, the coaching technology, key coaching skills and even the proven marketing strategies that work to fill your practice! Again, this course is completely free and there is no obligation, but reservations are required. (The course is not a sales pitch, by the way. We are very respectful.)

> *"It was a lot of fun taking the 1, 2, 3, Coach! TeleClass. The instructor was lively and interesting! I called her with questions between classes and she was very willing to spend the time talking with me. During the classes, the concepts of Irresistible Attraction and Eliminating Tolerations really spoke to me. It all made me want to learn more about this fascinating thing called coaching!"*
> *– Marilyn Hall, halls@intur.net*

> *"Before taking the 1, 2, 3, Coach! TeleClass, I was only vaguely interested in becoming a coach. But after the second class, during which the leader helped one of us make a major shift in only two minutes, I realized this was very powerful work and I wanted to learn how to*

do it. I started the enrollment process that very night. It was the right thing to have done. I love coaching and plan on being a coach for many years to come."
– Michael Sheffield, mscoach@sonic.net

For dates for 1,2,3, Coach! Classes, please call 1-800-48COACH or go to www.coachu.com.

C. Making It As A Coach TeleClass - one one-hour session
During this class you will learn the 10 most effective strategies for developing your practice and becoming the coach you know you are. The focus is mostly on the practical and marketing side, but you can also ask questions about how to deal with your concerns or fears about the transition and ramping up period and the various transition strategies that are available. The class is lead by a Coach U graduate who can provide both the encouragement and practical, reality-based answers that anyone considering the coaching field deserves. This class is suitable for someone who is just starting out or a professional seeking to transition into coaching. For the scheduled class dates, call 1-800-48COACH or go to www.coachu.com.

D. Live Coach Trainings
Coach U offers a road show as well, conducted in over 20 U.S. cities during 1999. Coaching Skills Weekends are designed to answer all your questions about becoming a coach or using a coach in your business or corporation. As well as answering your questions you walk away with some wonderful basic coaching skills that will be beneficial to you in any role you play in life. For the schedule, go to www.coachu.com.

"The Coaching Skills Weekends are incredibly rich and are wonderful opportunities to meet Coach U senior coaches as well as local coaches and hear about their experience developing their coaching practice and their thoughts on the Coach U program. The sessions are free and are offered throughout North America and Europe."
– Cynthia Bahnuik, Success Incorporated, cbahnuik@incentre.net

E. Coach U Annual Conferences
The annual Coach U conferences are designed not only to provide the opportunity to learn but the equally important opportunity to spend quality, creative time with like-minded and progressive-thinking colleagues. For information on upcoming events, call 1-800-48-COACH or visit the website and click on "conferences."

2. Making Your Choice
Here are some observations from some coaches that have made the choice:

"For several years I searched for solid 'coaching' skills training without much satisfaction. At one point in time I thought my only option was a Masters or Ph.D. in Counseling. But with those programs I'd have to complete many counseling courses before I could get skills training plus I have never wanted to be a therapist who deals with needy people. Coach U, from the beginning, provides solid skills training for dealing with healthy people problems."
– Marjorie Wall Hofer, leadercoach@usa.net

"I rarely make quick decisions and studied Coach U and the coaching process for about 18 months before taking the plunge. I tried 'lone ranger coaching' for about six months, but found myself too isolated and needing more than just the right attitude. I wanted information, community, instruction and mentors! I finally woke up one day saying, 'The time is now!' and enrolled that day. I am so glad I did...it is well worth the money!"
– Marilyn Hall, halls@intur.net

"I wasn't sure about enrolling in Coach U at first as I had spent so much money on seminars and training already. It turned out to be one of the best choices I have ever made. The program is so complete. Thomas has really written a fabulous program. But it doesn't stop with the 36 modules. The Coach U community of coaches is a family and every CTPer is made to feel a part of that family. Every single coach I have come to know is open and willing to share how they got started, any tools, words of inspiration, anything to help new coaches. If I never had a client, the personal growth and development I have received has been worth every penny and every minute. And I got a new 'extended family' in the package."
– Judy Irving, Uramiracle@aol.com

"My first year of coaching began on January 1st, 1998. I was interested in coaching part-time so I could travel with my husband now that my daughter has left home. I enrolled at Coach U and found a wonderful coach to work with. I took on a few pro bono clients and quickly began to feel like a real coach when my clients expressed how much our sessions were doing to move their lives forward. I got two coaching referral pages up on the Internet and designed a quick and easy web site. I kept my prices low as I was mostly concerned with getting a lot of experience. Now, by the end of the

year I have seven clients, many from the Internet, and have done a lot of traveling as well."
– Gail Valenti, lgvalenti@aol.com

"I have found that the process of transitioning to coaching is very individual. When I was ready, I quit my full-time job, before I had any paying clients. Not many people do it that way, but I had laid down a solid foundation and had my reserves in place. This way of changing worked best for me."
– Jo Ann Heiser, lifecoachjo@juno.com

"My first year at Coach U was tough. All of the agendas in my life became useless. I changed from wanting to get through the program to be certified to taking some classes for the second time to really integrate all of the concepts being presented. I found the Personal Foundation course very powerful early on. One year later I see myself as a different person. What I have to offer people is the experiential knowledge I have from my own development."
– Kathy Pike, kathyp@tesser.com, www.CoachKPike.com

"It's important to learn your way around the Coach U web site. But no need to get overwhelmed. Forget about trying to learn all the materials. You don't try to read all the books in your hometown library do you? Coaching is about people first.... Use the information you need. All the rest of it will be there when you need it. That's the beauty of it."
– Jay Perry, Jay@CoachingCollective.com, www.CoachingCollective.com

"The Coach U Web Page is a plethora of resources for learning about the world of coaching. It is always up-to-date and full of valuable information. I especially like the section on Special Interest Groups."
– Marilyn Hall, halls@intur.net

APPENDIX

TEAM 100 PROGRAM™ Version 3, 4/99

Helping clients get the results they need requires a team effort by the Coach and other professionals.

The **Team 100**™ List works like a dance card: You select the 100 other professionals who you want on your team. With the right players, here's what can happen:

- Your clients have access to a strong network.
- You can tap into high-expertise immediately.
- Most problems or needs can be solved, fast.
- Referrals start flowing among team members

How to Play:

1. Decide to get a full team within 1 year.
2. Fill in the team members you now know.
3. Start networking to fill in the other slots.
4. Pass around blank forms to associates.
5. Get yourself on other's **Team 100**™ lists.

C O A C H / U

Dedicated to the model of Networking: Sandy Vilas
Developed by the staff, trainers and participants of Coach U Inc.

Progress Chart

Date	Points (+/-)	Score
_____	_____	_____
_____	_____	_____
_____	_____	_____
_____	_____	_____
_____	_____	_____

TEAM 100 PROGRAM 100-Point Checklist
Sections

#	A	B	C	D	E
20					
19					
18					
17					
16					
15					
14					
13					
12					
11					
10					
9					
8					
7					
6					
5					
4					
3					
2					
1					

Give yourself credit as you get points from the 100-point program.
Fill in columns from the bottom up.

A. Biz & Work

Running a business, managing a career, finding work that you enjoy all come easier when you have experts and models to guide and inspire you.

○ New Business Specialist
Name: _____
Contact Info: _____

○ Career Consultant/Planner
Name: _____
Contact Info: _____

○ Graphic Artist
Name: _____
Contact Info: _____

○ Printer/Copy Place
Name: _____
Contact Info: _____

○ Turnaround Business Expert
Name: _____
Contact Info: _____

○ Corporate Trainer
Name: _____
Contact Info: _____

○ Professional Networker
Name: _____
Contact Info: _____

○ Internet Marketing Expert
Name: _____
Contact Info: _____

○ Web Presence Provider
Name: _____
Contact Info: _____

○ Personal Marketer
Name: _____
Contact Info: _____

○ Business Coach
Name: _____
Contact Info: _____

○ Corporate Coach
Name: _____
Contact Info: _____

○ Executive Coach
Name: _____
Contact Info: _____

○ Business Diagnostic Coach
Name: _____
Contact Info: _____

○ Marketing Coach
Name: _____
Contact Info: _____

○ Professional Writer
   Name: _____
   Contact Info: _____
○ Computer Consultant
   Name: _____
   Contact Info: _____
○ Hard Disk Crash Recoverer
   Name: _____
   Contact Info: _____
○ Software Consultant
   Name: _____
   Contact Info: _____
○ Headhunter
   Name: _____
   Contact Info: _____

___ **Number of items checked (20 max)**

B. Money & Legal
The only thing in the way of your financial independence is great advice and the willingness to apply it.

○ Small Business Attorney
   Name: _____
   Contact Info: _____
○ Real Estate Attorney
   Name: _____
   Contact Info: _____
○ Tax Attorney
   Name: _____
   Contact Info: _____
○ International Attorney
   Name: _____
   Contact Info: _____
○ Estate Attorney
   Name: _____
   Contact Info: _____
○ Copyright/Trademark Attorney
   Name: _____
   Contact Info: _____
○ Criminal Attorney
   Name: _____
   Contact Info: _____
○ Financial Planner
   Name: _____
   Contact Info: _____
○ Banker
   Name: _____
   Contact Info: _____

○ Realtor
Name: _____
Contact Info: _____

○ Venture Capitalist
Name: _____
Contact Info: _____

○ Stockbroker
Name: _____
Contact Info: _____

○ CPA
Name: _____
Contact Info: _____

○ Insurance - Life/Health/Disability
Name: _____
Contact Info: _____

○ Insurance - Liability
Name: _____
Contact Info: _____

○ Insurance - Home/Auto
Name: _____
Contact Info: _____

○ Bookkeeper/Bill Paying Service
Name: _____
Contact Info: _____

○ Grant Writer
Name: _____
Contact Info: _____

○ Property Manager
Name: _____
Contact Info: _____

○ Money Manager
Name: _____
Contact Info: _____

___ **Number of items checked (20 max)**

C. Personal & Health

Our bodies, minds and spirits can benefit from these experts.

○ MD - Internist
Name: _____
Contact Info: _____

○ MD - Ophthalmologist
Name: _____
Contact Info: _____

○ MD - Cosmetic Surgeon
Name: _____
Contact Info: _____

○ MD - Dermatologist
Name: _____
Contact Info: _____

○ MD - Sports
Name: _____
Contact Info: _____

○ MD - Psychiatrist
Name: _____
Contact Info: _____

○ Nutritionist
Name: _____
Contact Info: _____

○ ND (Naturopath)
Name: _____
Contact Info: _____

○ Massage Therapist
Name: _____
Contact Info: _____

○ Chiropractor
Name: _____
Contact Info: _____

○ Pharmacist
Name: _____
Contact Info: _____

○ Movement Therapist
Name: _____
Contact Info: _____

○ Acupuncturist
Name: _____
Contact Info: _____

○ Diagnostician
Name: _____
Contact Info: _____

○ Therapist - Depression
Name: _____
Contact Info: _____

○ Therapist - ADD Expert
Name: _____
Contact Info: _____

○ Therapist - Relationships
Name: _____
Contact Info: _____

○ Fertility Expert
Name: _____
Contact Info: _____

○ Dentist/Cosmetic Dentist
Name: _____
Contact Info: _____

○ Speech Therapist
  Name: _____
  Contact Info: _____

___ **Number of items checked (20 max)**

D. Personal Services
These are services that make our lives easier.

○ Housekeeping/Cleaning
  Name: _____
  Contact Info: _____
○ Travel Agent
  Name: _____
  Contact Info: _____
○ Event Planner
  Name: _____
  Contact Info: _____
○ Florist
  Name: _____
  Contact Info: _____
○ Professional Gift Service
  Name: _____
  Contact Info: _____
○ Portrait Photographer
  Name: _____
  Contact Info: _____
○ Caterer
  Name: _____
  Contact Info: _____
○ Seamstress/Tailor
  Name: _____
  Contact Info: _____
○ Childcare/Babysitter
  Name: _____
  Contact Info: _____
○ Minister/Clergy
  Name: _____
  Contact Info: _____
○ Auto mechanic/Car Care
  Name: _____
  Contact Info: _____
○ Electrician
  Name: _____
  Contact Info: _____
○ Air conditioning/Heating
  Name: _____
  Contact Info: _____

○ Plumber
    Name: _____
    Contact Info: _____

○ Professional Organizers
    Name: _____
    Contact Info: _____

○ Personal Concierge/Errands
    Name: _____
    Contact Info: _____

○ Dog Walker/Pet Sitter
    Name: _____
    Contact Info: _____

○ Good Book Maven
    Name: _____
    Contact Info: _____

○ Interior Designer/Decorator
    Name: _____
    Contact Info: _____

○ Handyman/woman
    Name: _____
    Contact Info: _____

___ **Number of items checked (20 max)**

E. Extreme Self Care

Extreme self-care refers to the practice of taking exceptionally good care of your body, mind and spirit. The professionals below can make a big difference in your emotional, physical and energy levels.

○ Skin Care Specialist/Spa
    Name: _____
    Contact Info: _____

○ Personal Assistant (Real)
    Name: _____
    Contact Info: _____

○ Personal Assistant (Virtual)
    Name: _____
    Contact Info: _____

○ Personal Trainer
    Name: _____
    Contact Info: _____

○ Healthy Food Delivery
    Name: _____
    Contact Info: _____

○ Personal Coach
    Name: _____
    Contact Info: _____

○ Spiritual Advisor/Clergy
Name: _____
Contact Info: _____

○ Manicurist/Pedicurist
Name: _____
Contact Info: _____

○ Jeweler
Name: _____
Contact Info: _____

○ Certified Rolfer
Name: _____
Contact Info: _____

○ Image/Color Consultant
Name: _____
Contact Info: _____

○ Personal Makeover Coach
Name: _____
Contact Info: _____

○ Communication Coach
Name: _____
Contact Info: _____

○ Feng Shui Consultant
Name: _____
Contact Info: _____

○ Reiki Master
Name: _____
Contact Info: _____

○ Alexander Technique Expert
Name: _____
Contact Info: _____

○ Irresistible Attraction Coach
Name: _____
Contact Info: _____

○ Visual Artist Consultant
Name: _____
Contact Info: _____

○ Lifestyle Design Coach
Name: _____
Contact Info: _____

○ Psychic
Name: _____
Contact Info: _____

___ **Number of items checked (20 max)**

Additional Team Member Ideas:
Elder Care specialist, Self-Defense Trainer, Dental Insurance, Pest Control, Retirement Planner, Home School Expert, Vet, Carpet Cleaner, Painter, Funeral Director, Decorator, Landscaper, Pediatrician, Architect, Optometrist, Grief Counselor, Strategic Planner, Pet Trainer, Holistic Medical Practitioner, Spiritual Healer, Development Disabilities, Personal Shopper.

International Team Member Ideas:
International Law Expert, Inter-Cultural Communicator (Diversity Trainer), International Travel Expert, Translator, Interpreter, Foreign Language Teacher, International Conference Coordinator.

Intellectual Property Notice:
This material and these concepts are the intellectual property of Coach U, Inc. You may not repackage or resell this program without express written authorization and royalty payment. The exception is that you may deliver this program to single individuals without authorization or fee. If you lead a workshop, develop or deliver a program to a group or company based on or including this material or these concepts, authorization and fees are required. You may make as many copies of this program as you wish, as long as you make no changes or deletions of any kind.

COACH U

Coach U, Inc.
P.O. Box 881595, Steamboat Springs, CO 80488-1595

1-800-48COACH • 1-800-FAX5655
info@coachu.com • http://www.coachu.com

JANE SMART Coach

Dear Colleague:

Hello. You are one of 100 friends, associates and colleagues to whom I am sending this letter. I am expanding my practice to include coaching and I wanted to let you know the types of clients I can do good work for and to ask you to be my partner in the development of my coaching practice.

I have enclosed some material on the nature of coaching, but briefly, as a coach, I:

1. Help my clients set larger, better, more rewarding personal and professional goals.
2. Speak with each client at least weekly to help them strategize and take action.
3. Ask more of my clients than they – or others – might ask of themselves.

The roles of the coach include: Mentor, Consultant and Success Partner.

As you know, I have been a business management consultant for 11 years. By adding this coaching service and weaving in the coaching success principles, structures and technology, I can do far more for my clients than before.

I am currently working with six coaching clients and my practice goal is to be working with 36 clients. I do not advertise, but rely instead on my current clients and my colleagues, like you, for referrals.

My specialty is working with the following types of clients:

1. The Entrepreneur who is ready to at least double his or her business, quickly.
2. The Consultant who wishes to expand his/her practice significantly.
3. The CEO or Executive who needs to bring his or her organization to the next level.

I charge $250 per month for a weekly session. Clients out of the area may use my 800 Coaching Line.

Will you help? I am asking that you keep me in mind when you run across anyone who is one of the three types listed above. Also, if you know someone who you think would benefit from coaching – perhaps, even yourself – I am happy to spend 30 minutes with them to see if I can help or by putting them in touch with one my coaching colleagues who I think can do a great job for them. (There are over 7,000 coaches in the US, I am in touch with 150 of these, who are part of a training program offered through Coach U.)

I have enclosed several business cards. Please share these, or even ask me to call someone who has expressed an interest. And, please let me know how I can help you!

Warmest regards,

Jane Smart
Coach

B

CONTENTS OF COACH U
Reference Library

2600 pages

Welcome Kit
Forms Book 1 - Client Welcome Package (F1)
Forms Book 2 - Assessments Test (F2)
Forms Book 3 - Client Forms & Worksheets (F3)
Forms Book 4 - Client Articles (F4)
Forms Book 5 - Practice & Client Management (F5)
Forms Book 6 - Articles & Handouts for the Coach (F6)
Personal Foundation Program (E2)
25 Secrets of Extreme Profitability (A3)
Irresistible Attraction (E3)
Attraction Program (E3)
25 Secrets of Having the Life you Really Want (A1)
The Coaching Skills Book (A2)
X1 Biz Builder TeleClass (no tab)
X2 Personal Foundation TeleClass (E2)
Seven Secrets of Coaching Anyone - T1 (A7)
The Coaching Distinctionary (A4)
Transitioning to Full-Time Coaching (A6)
C Modules
C1 Client Typing TeleClass (C1)
C2 Listening TeleClass (C2)
C3 Personal Coaching TeleClass (C3)
C4 Business Coaching TeleClass (C4)
C5 Client Success TeleClass (C5)
C6 Coach Success TeleClass (C6)
C7 Empowering TeleClass (C7)
C8 Advising TeleClass (C8)
C9 Relating TeleClass (C9)
C10 Developing TeleClass (C10)
C11 Strategizing TeleClass (C11)
C12 Challenging TeleClass (C12)
C13 Life Planning TeleClass (C13)
C14 Personal Path TeleClass (C14)
C15 Spiritual Path TeleClass (C15)
C16 Buff TeleClass (C16)
C17 Advanced Personal Development TeleClass (C17)
C18 Financial Independence TeleClass (C18)
C19 The Professional TeleClass (C19)
C20 The Restorative Client TeleClass (C20)
C21 The Entrepreneur TeleClass (C21)
C22 The Manager TeleClass (C22)
C23 The CEO Executive TeleClass (C23)
C24 Other Client Types TeleClass (C24)
C25 New Business Success TeleClass (C25)
C26 Marketing for the New Millenium TeleClass (C26)
C27 Small Biz Success TeleClass (C27)
C28 Business Turnarounds TeleClass (C28)

C

C29 Profitability TeleClass (C29)
C30 Organization Development TeleClass (C30)
C31 Attracting Clients TeleClass (C31)
C32 Closing The Sale TeleClass (C32)
C33 Client Management TeleClass (C33)
C34 Practice Management TeleClass (C34)
C35 Full Practice TeleClass (C35)
C36 New Markets TeleClass (C36)

CLEAN SWEEP PROGRAM™ Version 3, 4/99

You have more natural energy when you are clear with your environment, health and emotional balance, money and relationships.

The **Clean Sweep** Program consists of 100 items which, when completed, give you the vitality and strength you want.

The program can be completed in less than one year.

Instructions for this assessment
are on the last page.

Developed by the staff, trainers and participants of Coach U, Inc.

Date	Progress Chart Points (+/-)	Score
_____	_____	_____
_____	_____	_____
_____	_____	_____
_____	_____	_____

D

CLEAN SWEEP PROGRAM **100-Point Checklist** Sections					
#	A	B	C	D	E
25					
24					
23					
22					
21					
20					
19					
18					
17					
16					
15					
14					
13					
12					
11					
10					
9					
8					
7					
6					
5					
4					
3					
2					
1					

Give yourself credit as you get points from the 100-point program.
Fill in columns from the bottom up.

PHYSICAL ENVIRONMENT

- ○ My personal files, papers and receipts are neatly filed away.
- ○ My car is in excellent condition. (Doesn't need mechanical work, repairs, cleaning or replacing)
- ○ My home is neat and clean. (Vacuumed, closets clean, desks and tables clear, furniture in good repair; windows clean)
- ○ My appliances, machinery and equipment work well. (Refrigerator, toaster, snow-blower, water heater, toys)
- ○ My clothes are all pressed, clean and make me look great. (No wrinkles, baskets of laundry, torn, out-of-date or ill-fitting clothes)
- ○ My plants and animals are healthy. (Fed, watered, getting light and love)
- ○ My bed/bedroom lets me have the best sleep possible. (Firm bed, light, air)
- ○ I live in a home/apartment that I love.
- ○ I surround myself with beautiful things.
- ○ I live in the geographic area I choose.
- ○ There is ample and healthy light around me.
- ○ I consistently have adequate time, space and freedom in my life.
- ○ I am not damaged by my environment.
- ○ I am not tolerating anything about my home or work environment.
- ○ My work environment is productive and inspiring. (Synergistic, ample tools and resources; no undue pressure)
- ○ I recycle.
- ○ I use non ozone-depleting products.
- ○ My hair is the way I want it.
- ○ I surround myself with music which makes my life more enjoyable.
- ○ My bed is made daily.
- ○ I don't injure myself, or bump into things.
- ○ People feel comfortable in my home.
- ○ I drink purified water.
- ○ I have nothing around the house or in storage that I do not need.
- ○ I am consistently early or easily on time.

____ **Number of checked items (25 max)**

HEALTH & EMOTIONAL BALANCE

- ○ I rarely use caffeine. (Chocolate, coffee, colas, tea) less than 3 times per week, total.

- ○ I rarely eat sugar. (Less than 3 times per week.)
- ○ I rarely watch television. (Less than 5 hours per week)
- ○ I rarely drink alcohol. (Less than 2 drinks per week)
- ○ My teeth and gums are healthy. (Have seen dentist in last 6 months)
- ○ My cholesterol count is healthful.
- ○ My blood pressure is healthful.
- ○ I have had a complete physical exam in the past 3 years.
- ○ I do not smoke tobacco or other substances.
- ○ I do not use illegal drugs or misuse prescribed medications.
- ○ I have had a complete eye exam within the past two years. (Glaucoma check, vision test)
- ○ My weight is within my ideal range.
- ○ My nails are healthy and attractive.
- ○ I don't rush or use adrenaline to get the job done.
- ○ I have a rewarding life beyond my work or profession.
- ○ I have something to look forward to virtually every day.
- ○ I have no habits which I find to be unacceptable.
- ○ I am aware of the physical or emotional problems or conditions I have, and I am now fully taking care of all of them.
- ○ I consistently take evenings, weekends and holidays off and take at least two weeks of vacation each year.
- ○ I have been tested for the AIDS antibody.
- ○ I use well-made sunglasses.
- ○ I do not suffer.
- ○ I floss daily.
- ○ I walk or exercise at least three times per week.
- ○ I hear well.

____ **Number of checked items (25 max)**

MONEY

- ○ I currently save at least 10% of my income.
- ○ I pay my bills on time, virtually always.
- ○ My income source/revenue base is stable and pre-dictable.
- ○ I know how much I must have to be minimally financially independent and I have a plan to get there.
- ○ I have returned or made-good-on any money I bor-rowed.
- ○ I have written agreements and am current with payments to individuals or companies to whom I owe money.
- ○ I have 6 months' living expenses in a money market-type account.
- ○ I live on a weekly budget which allows me to save and not suffer.

○ All my tax returns have been filed and all my taxes have been paid.
○ I currently live well, within my means.
○ I have excellent medical insurance.
○ My assets (car, home, possessions, treasures) are well-insured.
○ I have a financial plan for the next year.
○ I have no legal clouds hanging over me.
○ My will is up-to-date and accurate.
○ Any parking tickets, alimony or child support are paid and current.
○ My investments do not keep me awake at night.
○ I know how much I am worth.
○ I am on a career/professional/business track which is or will soon be financially and personally rewarding.
○ My earnings are commensurate with the effort I put into my job.
○ I have no "loose ends" at work.
○ I am in relationship with people who can assist in my career/professional development.
○ I rarely miss work due to illness.
○ I am putting aside enough money each month to reach financial independence.
○ My earnings outpace inflation, consistently.

____ **Number of checked items (25 max)**

RELATIONSHIPS

○ I have told my parents, in the last 3 months, that I love them.
○ I get along well with my sibling(s).
○ I get along well with my co-workers/clients.
○ I get along well with my manager/staff.
○ There is no one who I would dread or feel uncomfortable "running across" (in the street, at an airport or party).
○ I put people first and results second.
○ I have let go of the relationships which drag me down or damage me. ("Let go" means to end, walk away from, state, handle, no longer be attached to.)
○ I have communicated or attempted to communicate with everyone who I have damaged, injured or seriously disturbed, even if it wasn't fully my fault.
○ I do not gossip or talk about others.
○ I have a circle of friends/family who love and appreciate me for who I am, more than just what I do for them.
○ I tell people how they can satisfy me.
○ I am fully caught up with letters and calls.
○ I always tell the truth, no matter what.

○ I receive enough love from people around me to feel good.
○ I have fully forgiven those people who have hurt/damaged me, deliberate or not.
○ I am a person of his/her word; people can count on me.
○ I quickly clear miscommunications and misunderstandings when they do occur.
○ I live life on my terms, not by the rules or preferences of others.
○ There is nothing unresolved with past loves or spouses.
○ I am in tune with my wants and needs and get them taken care of.
○ I do not judge or criticize others.
○ I do not "take personally" the things that people say to me.
○ I have a best friend or soul-mate.
○ I state requirements rather than complain.
○ I spend time with people who don't try to change me.

_____ **Number of checked items (25 max)**

INSTRUCTIONS

There are 4 steps to completing the Clean Sweep™ Program.

Step 1
Answer each question. If true, check the box. Be rigorous; be a hard grader. If the statement is sometimes or usually true please DO NOT check the box until the statement is virtually always true for you. (No "credit" until it is really true!) If the statement does not apply to you, check the box. If the statement will never be true for you, check the box. (You get "credit" for it because it does not apply or will never happen.) And, you may change any statement to fit your situation better.

Step 2
Summarize each section. Add up the number of True boxes for each of the 4 sections and write those amounts where indicated. Then add up all four sections and write the current total in the box on the front of this form.

Step 3
Color in the Progress Chart on the front page. Always start from the bottom up. The goal is to have the entire chart filled in. In the meantime, you will have a current picture of how you are doing in each of the four areas.

Step 4
Keep playing until all boxes are filled in. You can do it! This process may take 30 or 360 days, but you can achieve a Clean Sweep! Use your coach or a friend to assist you. And check back once a year for maintenance.

BENEFITS

On the lines below, jot down specific benefits, results and shifts which happen in your life because you handled an item in the **Clean Sweep** Program.

Date   Benefit

_____

_____

_____

_____

Fill in the bar chart on the front panel as you increase your
Clean Sweep scores.

Coach U, Inc.
P.O. Box 881595
Steamboat Springs, CO 80488-1595

1-800-48COACH • 1-800-FAX5655
info@coachu.com • http://www.coachu.com

COUNTRIES IN WHICH COACH U
Has Students and/or Graduates

Australia
Austria
Bahamas
Belgium
Bermuda
Canada
Columbia
Cyprus
Denmark
Finland
France
Germany
Holland
Hong Kong
Indonesia
Ireland
Israel
Italy
Jamaica
Japan
Kenya
Malaysia
Netherlands
New Zealand
Norway
Singapore
South Africa
Spain
Sweden
Switzerland
United Arab
Virgin Islands
United Kingdom
United States

E

COACHING SPECIALITIES

As the demand for coaching grows, so too does the demand for coaching specialties.

Below is a list of 101 Coaching Specialties, many of which have already become popular. So, whether you are a coach in training wondering what the specialty options are or you are a client seeking a specialist, the following list should be very useful. Note: Some specialties require special licensing/testing by states or countries. Others require advanced training, qualifications and testing. Finally, some specialties are just now being popularized.

1. Corporate

Corporate Coach
Executive/CEO Coach
Organizational Development Coach
Management Coach
Culture/Paradigm Shift Coach
Leadership Coach
Board of Directors' Coach
Human Resource Coach
Quality/TQM Coach
Staff/Employee Coach

2. Marketing/Sales

Sales Coach
Public Relations Coach
Marketing Coach
Brand Management Coach
Promotions Coach
Pricing Strategy Coach
Buzz-Development Coach
Advertising Coach
Direct Marketing Coach
Personal Marketing Coach

3. Small Business

New Business Coach
Entrepreneur Coach
Business Turnaround Coach
MLM/Network Marketing Coach
Networking Coach
Budgeting/Planning Coach
Business Financial Coach
Mission Development Coach
Marketing Coach
Partner's Coach

F

4. Relationships

Marriage Coach
Family Coach
Romance Coach
Team Coach
Parent Coach
Love Coach
Divorce Recovery Coach
Couples' Coach
Network Development Coach
Intimacy Coach

5. Lifestage/Lifestyle

Fresh Start Coach
Generation X Coach
Baby Boomer Coach
Retirement Coach
Lifestyle Design Coach
Teen Coach
Students' Coach
Workaholics' Coach
Transition Coach
Personal Turnaround Coach

6. Quality of Life

Nutrition/Diet Coach
Exercise /Fitness Coach
Vegan/Vegetarian Coach
Recreation Coach
Travel/Adventure Coach
Wellness Coach
Energy/Reiki Coach
Makeover Coach
Buff /Style Coach
Stress Reduction Coach

7. Success Coach

Motivation/Edge Coach
Goals/Results Coach
Idea/Creativity Coach
Problem-solving/Solution Coach
Time Management/Leverage Coach
Strategic Coach
Attraction/OS Coach
Financial/Money Coach
Career Coach
Legacy/Achievement Coach

8. Special Markets

Consultants/Coaches' Coach
MDs/Health Professional/Dental Coach
Attorney/Law Firm Coach
CPA/Financial Service Professional Coach
Trainers/Speakers' Coach
Gay/Lesbian Coach
Single Parents' Coach
Realtors/Real Estate Coach
Therapists/Counselors' Coach
Ministers/Caregivers Coach

9. Personal Development

12-step/Recovery/Addiction Coach
Personal Foundation Coach
Integrity Coach
Balance Coach
Co-dependency Coach
Fear Coach
Post-12-step Coach
Resolution Coach
Attainments Coach
Spiritual Coach

10. Special Skills & Situations

Communication Coach
Cyber Coach
Internet/Web Coach
Diagnostic Coach
Futurist Coach
Language/Phrasing Coach
Learning Coach
Software/Computer Coach
Writing Coach
Personal Organization Coach

And ...
General Practitioner Coach

NUGGET CATEGORIES

Coach U has a collection of thousands of knowledge nuggets for business, personal development, professional coaching and fun. Knowledge nuggets contain rich information, inspiring quotes, useful tips and helpful solutions to everyday needs and special problems. These knowledge nuggets come in several types, including Coaching Tips, Distinctions, Quotations, Tidbits and Top Ten Lists.   These are the categories of the knowledge nuggets.

Business

Entrepreneurs, Small Business, Home Office
Careers
Corporate, Organizational Issues, Competition
Professional, MD, JD, CPA, Therapist, Consultant
Management, Staff Development, Projects, Delegation, Leadership
Sales, Marketing, PR, Sales Management
Effectiveness Skills, Results
Future, Strategic Planning, Leverage Opportunities
Non-profit Organizations, Governmental Agencies
Business Administration, Operations
Business Relationships, Networking, Relating
Internet, Web, Electronic Systems
Profitability, Viability, Revenue, Pricing, Cash Flow
Customers, Customer Service, R&D
Real Estate only– Realtors, Brokers, Managers, Executives
Business Communication Skills
Network Marketing, Multilevel Marketing, Amway
Virtual Education, Distance Learning, Electronic Training
Speaking, Writers, Presenters, Trainers

Personal

Personal Development: Basic
Relationships, Relating, Couples
Spirituality, Awareness, Path, Energy, Flow, Consciousness
Success, Smart Choices, Wisdom
Emotional Healing, Recovery, Coping, 12-Step
Health, Well-Being, Self-Care, Diet, Balance, Eating
Symptoms/Signs of Problems, Conditions, Addictions, Behavior
Money, Financial
Quality of Life Ideas
Personal Foundation
Irresistible Attraction
Life Skills
Religion
Communication Skills, Language, Expression
Stages in Life, Major Changes, Teens, Retirement,

G

Marriage, Divorce
The Ultimate Changes
Parenting, Family Issues
Reasons Why, Clues to Behavior Patterns
Personal Network of Professionals, Services
Shifts to Make, Changing Behavior
Consumer, Buying, Purchasing, Suggestions
Book Summaries
WORDZ: Fun with vocabulary building
Humor, Jokes, Trivia, Miscellaneous
Trends, Future, Paradigms
Miscellaneous/Top Ten Site Administration

Coaching and Coach Training
Becoming a Coach
Coach U: Information
Coach U: 1, 2, 3, Coach TeleClass
Coach U - Public Information for Students
Coach Success, Marketing, Full Practice
Special Markets for Coaches
Coaching Tools and Skills
Situations/Situational Advice
TeleClass Leadership, Coach Trainers, Trainer Team
About coaching, potential clients, coach marketing
Coach U Success, Improvement, Marketing
Coach Effectiveness, Improvement
Thomas Leonard
Tele-University
Personal Foundation
Coaching Secrets
Distinctions: A superb coaching tool

Coach U Students (CTP Members Only)
General Guidance, Coach Training Program
Module Workbook Supplements
Contextual Points for CTP Modules
Distinctions for CTP Modules
Field Work Assignments for CTP Modules
Learning Objectives for CTP Modules
Coaching Mistakes to Avoid for CTP Modules

Symptom > Situation > Source > Solution > Shift

1. Recognize all of the Symptoms
- Look/listen for action and inaction, verbal and nonverbal communication, results and lack of results
- Symptoms are what you can see, feel or hear; many may be subtle and require training.

2. Size up the Situation and give it a label
- Symptoms point to one or more types of situations.
- When you give it a label, you can coach from "knowing" what's really going on.

3. Discern the Source of the Symptoms
- The source is why the symptom is occurring; the explanation, reason, or cause.
- Once the source is known, the coach gives direction to resolve source vs. Band-Aid symptom.

4. Provide the Solution
- The coaching solution may include: awareness, action, direction, distinction, formula, language.
- There is always a solution if you know the source; however, the client may not wish to solve it.

5. Focus the client on Shift while the Solution is occuring
- Shifts make the solution permanent vs. temporary.
- If you've done your solution properly, the client will naturally shift (but you can still share it).

H

MEDIA COVERAGE

- *ABC's "American Journal", <u>Using A Coach for Your Dream Career</u>, 1998*
- *Accounting for Law Firms, <u>A coach for the firm</u>? by Moira Jamieson, April 1997 ♣*
- *Adler Online Show, August 16, 1996*
- *Alaska Airlines Magazine, <u>Sporting Edge</u> by H. Phillips Hoffman, Nov. 1996 ♣*
- *Albuquerque Journal, Sage Magazine, <u>Making dreams come true: A personal life coach can keep you on target in advancing from point A to point B</u> by Susan Stiger, May 1997 ♣*
- *Ambassador (TWA inflight magazine), <u>Called for Goaltending</u> by Bennett Davis, November, 1996 #*
- *American Medical News, Jan. 5, 1998*
- *Anchorage Daily News, 1998*
- *Apple's Web Page <u>Small Business Tools</u>, Aug. 1996*
- *Asbury Park Press, <u>Coaches that get you back in the game</u> by Robert Hordt, May 1998 ♣*
- *BBC, Sept. 9, 1996*
- *Bloomberg Personal, <u>Support from the Sidelines: Financial coaches - a New Age mix of therapist, educator, and bean counter - help the confused gain confidence</u> by Richard Bierck, March, 1998 ♣*
- *Boca Raton Business Journal, by Don Hunziker, March 10, 1997 ♣*
- *Boston Globe, <u>Personal "trainers" find business niche: Clients cite gains from career coaches</u> by Sacha Pfeiffer, Dec. 1, 1996 ♣*
- *Boston Globe, <u>Rent-a-mentor coaxes their success: Business coach finds a market</u> by Stacy Milbouer, June 14, 1998 ♣*
- *Boston Herald, August 1996*
- *Bottomline Business*
- *Boulder Daily Camera, "<u>Executive coaches" help businesses reach new heights</u> by Carly Schulaka ♣*
- *Boulder Daily Planet, <u>Advisors create game plan for living</u> by Thomas May, March 12, 1997 ♣*
- *Business 96 (Wells Fargo bank customer magazine), <u>We coach - you win</u>, Oct./Nov., 1996 ♣*
- *Business 98, <u>How to use a "coach" - part consultant, part mentor - to give your business the winning edge</u> by Alan Naditz, Dec./Jan. 1998 ♣*
- *Business Journal (Charlotte), <u>Business embraces coaching: Mentor relationships bolster performance, reduce mistakes</u> by Edward Martin ♣*
- *Business Strategies, <u>Executives find success using per-*

sonal coaches by Betty Adams, Jan. 1997 ❖
- *Canadian Business, Have your coach call my coach: For a mere $500 or so a month, you too can have your very own mentor* by David North, June, 1997 ❖
- *Career Explorer*
- *Career Planning and Adult Development Journal, early 1998*
- *Cary News, Business Profile: DJ Mitsch* by Jane Farmer Paige, March 9, 1996 ✧
- *CBC Newsworld radio*
- *CBS This Morning, March 1996*
- *CFO, Your own personal Vince Lombardi: How a new breed of professional confidants helps CFOs shape up* by Joseph McCafferty, Nov. 1996 ❖
- *Charlotte Observer, Sept. 1996*
- *Chicago Tribune (columnist), May 1996*
- *Chicago Tribune, Looking for answers? Perhaps it's time you grabbed a seat in the coach's corner* by Connie Lauerman, Jan. 22, 1997 ❖
- *Chicago Tribune, You, too, can have a Bela Karolyi of your very own* by Mary Schmich, March 13, 1998 ❖
- *Chicago Tribune, Personal coach can make you a winner* by Carol Kleiman, May 17, 1998 ❖
- *Cincinnati Post, Coaches for life: Motivators help clients meet goals* by Camilla Warrick, Dec. 19, 1996 ❖
- *CIO, Personal coaches...as long as they don't make you do jumping jacks* by Derek Slater, Nov. 1, 1997 ❖
- *Cleveland Plain-Dealer, March 1996*
- *CNBC Money Matters (4 minutes), June 1996*
- *CNBC, Steals and Deals Show (3 minutes), Feb. 1996*
- *CNN Impact, Dec. 27, 1997, April 19-20, 1998*
- *CNN TV/Australia, Feb. 1996*
- *Comedy Central/Politically Incorrect, February 1996*
- *Common Boundary magazine, Coaches for life* by Lynda McCullough, Jan./Feb. 1996 ❖
- *Controller, A coach of your own* by Shari Caudron, Dec. 1997 ❖
- *Corporate Detroit Magazine*
- *CTV News/BCTV News (Canada), Feb. 1996*
- *Customer Service Coach, Sept. 1996*
- *Daily South Sider (Chicago), Life coaches...Business and personal training helps clients champion their dreams, April 21, 1998*
- *Daily Southtown (suburban Chicago), 1998*
- *Dallas Morning News, Setting priorities: Personal coaches help clients get what they want* by Camille Kraeplin, July 3, 1995 ❖
- *DBA Magazine (Houston), November 1996*
- *Denver Post, Businesses hire coaches to build winning*

  teams by Robert Schwab Oct. 18, 1998 ✧
- Denver Post, _Shape up career with "coach:" Job inse-curity feeds demand for New Age mentors_ by Ann Rovin, April 1996 ✧ ♣
- Denver Reporter-Herald, _Personal coaches help get clients off the bench and into the game_ by Hank Rosenblum, Aug. 17-18, 1996 ♣
- Des Moines Business Record, Aug. 26, 1996
- Detroit Free Press, _The voice of experience is as close as the phone: Business coaches sell their wisdom_ by Nancy Costello, March 17, 1998 ♣
- Detroit Metro Times, _Training for the Top: Workers are turning to personal coaches to kick them into gear_ by Jane Slaughter, June 11-17, 1997 ♣
- Dividends (Staples' customer magazine), Jan. 1997
- Donahue Show, July 1996
- Dover-Sherborn (MA) Suburban Press, June 25, 1996
- Drew Magazine (Drew Univ. alumni), _Soul Trainer_ (profile of coach Jim Vuocolo) by Robin Wallace, Summer 1997 ♣
- Eastside Journal, _Personal business coaches help workers achieve their goals_ by Eric Zoeckler, _Taming the Workplace_ columnist, March 4, 1997 ♣
- EDS website - www.eds.com _HEAD GAMES - See how an executive coach can help you pump up your career_ by Ursula Marinelli, July 1999 ✧
- Enter Magazine (www.entermag.com), 1996
- Enterprising Women, _Business coaching: A key to balance and success_ by Dee
- Helfgott, Sept./Oct. 1996 ♣
- Entrepreneur Magazine, August 1996
- Entrepreneur, December 1996
- Essence, _Valerie Williams on managing stress in start-ups_, July 1997 ♣
- Executive Female, _How a coach can help you be a better manager_ by Monci Williams, Jan./Feb., 1997 ♣
- Executive Update
- Family Circle, Aug. 1996
- Family Therapy Networker, _Breaking Free: Career Change as a Liberating Experience_ by Mary Sykes Wylie, Jan./Feb., 1998 ♣
- Fast Company, _Wanna be a player? Get a coach!_ by Claire Tristram, Oct./Nov. 1996 ♣
- Female Executive Magazine, September 1995
- Fortune, _Don't blow your new job_, June 22, 1998
- Ft. Lauderdale Sun Sentinel, _Need a Clue about Life? Hire a coach_ by Sherry Windston, Feb. 26, 1996 ✧
- Gannett News, by Mitch Broder, May, 1998
- Hartford Business Journal, August 1996

- *Harvard Business Review, <u>The executive as coach: The goal of coaching is the goal of good management: to make the most of an organization's valuable resources</u> by James Waldroop and Timothy Butler, Nov. - Dec. 1996* ✤
- *Harvard Resource Newspaper, Feb. 1996*
- *Healthfile (syndicated health news service), <u>What's your motivation? If you need help getting fit, a date or just putting your life on track, just hire a coach to whip you into shape</u> by Margaret Littman, Sept., 1997* ✤
- *High School Magazine, <u>What can we learn from professional coaches</u>? by Damian Nash, March/April 1998* ✤
- *Houston Business Journal, July 1996*
- *Houston Chronicle, <u>Coaches help put business, life in better shape</u> by L.M. Sixel, Feb. 1996* ✧
- *Houston Chronicle, July 1994*
- *HQ (Australia), <u>Kick my butt</u> by Tessa Souter, July/Aug. 1997* ✤
- *HR Briefing (published by The Bureau of Business Practice), June 25, 1998*
- *Income Opportunities Magazine, July 1996*
- *Indianapolis Business Journal, <u>Execs call coaches for career tune-ups: Trendy advisors catching on</u> by Stephen Beaven, Dec. 23-19, 1996* ✤
- *Industry Week, <u>Hire a Coach? Executive coaches are like a business consultant, weekly squash partner and spouse all rolled into one</u> by Shari Caudron, Oct. 21, 1996* ✤
- *Infoworld, <u>Could you use a coach? Professional guidance can aid personal and career development</u> by Deborah DeVoe, May 24, 1999* ✧
- *Internet World, <u>Career Coaches See Internet As Tool for Counseling Clients. E-mail used to advise workers about job searching, skill building</u> by Kathleen Murphy, Sept. 14, 1998* ✧
- *JobSmart, <u>Getting a little push: Specialized services can create a whole new you for the workplace</u> by Jim Woodworth, Sept. 1, 1998* ✤
- *Keynoter, Feb. 1997*
- *Kiplinger's Personal Finance, <u>Hire a coach to shape up your life? The game plan is to reduce family stress</u> by Robert Frick, March 1997* ✤
- *Kiplinger Report, The (Kiplinger's TV show), Fall 1997*
- *KMPC 710 AM Los Angeles, October 1996*
- *Knight-Ridder Newspapers, <u>The personal touch: Coaches: Boomers find their center by hiring advisers to seek with them</u> by James A. Fussell, May 1998*
- *Las Vegas Review-Journal, <u>Personal Coaches Bring Goals Into Focus</u> by Marian Green, March 18, 1996*

- *Las Vegas Sun, <u>Business Coaches: Consultants for the '90s</u> by Pauline Bell, March 18, 1996* ✧
- *Lawyer's Weekly USA, <u>A career coach can boost your profits, improve your life</u> by Bill Ibelle, Feb. 1997* ✤
- *London Times, <u>A word in your ear: She's mother, friend, therapist all in one and charges by the hour</u> by Tessa Souter, March 22, 1997* ✤
- *Long Island Newspaper, <u>Virtual Coach Offers Advice, But For A Price</u> by Patricia Kitchen, 3/17/96* ✧
- *Los Angeles Times, <u>Part Therapist, Part Management Consultant</u> by David Rani, May 1994* ✧
- *Los Angeles Times, <u>Putting a Coach In Your Corner</u> by Carol Smith, May 20, 1996* ✧
- *Mademoiselle, <u>Be Your Own Career Coach</u> by Maxine Paetro, March, 1997* ✤
- *Management Review (American Management Association), <u>Executive coaches call the plays</u> by Gail Dutton, Feb. 1997* ✤
- *Manchester Union Leader, <u>From Coach U to coaching you</u>, May 26, 1997* ✤
- *Meetings & Conventions, <u>All the right moves/managing your career</u> by Dana Nigro, Oct. 1997* ✤
- *Meetings & Conventions, <u>Coaching the Office Boor</u> by Marc Boisclair, Oct. 1996* ✤
- *Men's Fitness, Jan. 1997*
- *Miami Herald, <u>The Game of Life now Comes with Coaches: Personal motivator takes traditional roles, rolls them into one</u> by Lydia Martin, March 6, 1996* ✧
- *Miami Herald, May 1993*
- *Milwaukee Business Journal, <u>Coaches advise professionals, entrepreneurs,</u> by Robert Mullins, April 12, 1999* ✧
- *Modern Salon, 1998*
- *Money, <u>A coach may be the guardian angel you need to rev up your career</u> by Karen Hube, Dec. 1996* ✤
- *Money, <u>Live your dream</u> by Andrea Rock, Dec. 1997* ✤
- *Montreal Gazette, July 1996*
- *NBC Nightly News, Leading Edge Segment (4 minutes), Feb. 1996*
- *New Age Journal, <u>Living your dreams: To follow your bliss, you may need a new kind of consultant - a life coach. It's like hiring</u> Nov/Dec 1996*
- *New Jersey Star-Ledger, <u>Companies cultivate advisers</u> by Ellen Simon, Jan. 26, 1997* ✤
- *New Mexican, <u>Holding Hands, Kicking Butts</u> by Hollis Walker* ✧
- *New Mexican, June 1996*
- *New York Times, <u>Achieving success with the help of a coach</u> by Penny Singer, Sept. 14, 1997* ✤

I-4

- *New York Times, <u>Personal Trainers to Buff the Boss's People Skills</u> by Trip Gabriel, May 1996* ✧
- *Newburyport Herald, <u>Film focuses on improving quality of life</u> by Sarah P. Jones* ✧
- *News 12 Long Island, Sept. 6, 1996*
- *Newsday, <u>Virtual Coach Offers Advice, But for a Price</u> by Patricia Kitchen, <u>Fast Track</u> columnist, March 17, 1996* ♣
- *Newsday, April 1996*
- *Newstrack Executive Tape Service, Sept. 1996*
- *Newsweek, Feb. 5, 1996*
- *NPR's WAMC, <u>Vox Pop</u> show (aired in the NY, MA, VT area), 1998*
- *Office Hours*
- *<u>On the Job</u> column, syndicated by ParadigmTSA (www.paradigm-TSA.com), <u>Does Your Career Need a Coach</u>? by Evan Cooper, July 1999* ✧
- *Optimist, Fall 1996*
- *Orange County Register, <u>Coaching from sidelines: Corporations are drawing on the experience of outside advisers</u> by Jan Norman, July 28, 1997* ♣
- *Oregonian, <u>New Players in the Corporate Game</u> by Roger Crockett, May 19, 1996* ✧
- *Orlando Sentinel, <u>A coach for your career</u> by Linda Shrieves, April 19, 1996* ✧
- *Orlando Sentinel, <u>Be a player. Get a coach</u>. By Michael McLeod, July 18, 1999* ✧
- *Ottawa Citizen, March 1996*
- *Pacific Sun, <u>Hired help: Need motivation? Personal and professional coaches can goad you to success</u> by Nikki Meredith, Sept. 24, 1996* ♣
- *Palm Beach Daily News, Oct. 1993*
- *Palm Beach Post, <u>Find out what you love to do and then do it</u> by Jim Pawlak, Nov. 17, 1996*
- *Palm Beach Post, June 1994*
- *PBS, McQuisition Show, Oct. 1995*
- *Phoenix Sun, <u>Hey Coach! Help Me Make the Big Plays in Life</u> by Alexis Brown, March 1996* ✧
- *Pioneer Press (MN), <u>Coaching vs. mentoring</u> by Amy Gage, Staff columnist, April 11, 1999* ✧
- *Portland Business Journal, Aug. 30, 1996*
- *PR Reporter, <u>The Emerging Field of Coaching: What Exactly Coaches Do</u>, May 25, 1998* ♣
- *Practice Strategies, Sept. 1996*
- *Press Publications, <u>Personal coaching It's not about sports; it's an approach to managing life</u> By Cheryl Price, April 12, 1996* ✧
- *Purchasing Today, <u>A career fitness evaluation</u> by Carolyn Pye, Feb. 1997* ♣

- *Radio New Zealand, Feb. 1996*
- *Raleigh, NC News & Observer, <u>Coaching for keeps - Career coaching is a growth business, spawned by people's need for workplace guidance – and a willingness to pay for it</u> by Laura Wenzel, March 28, 1999* ✧
- *Redbook, <u>The 3 Best Secrets of Life Coaches</u>, Feb., 1998*
- *Registered Representative, <u>Getting a Coach: Raising your practice to a higher level may require the expertise of a coach</u> by Dom Del Prete, Feb. 1997* ♣
- *Report on Business Magazine, <u>Coach in the corner office</u> by Tracy Johnson, Sept. 1997* ♣
- *Rochester Democrat and Chronicle, <u>Coaches sell selves as mentor, friend, consultant</u> by Kathleen Driscoll, March 30, 1996* ♣
- *Rolling Stone, Oct. 1996*
- *Rotarian, 1998*
- *San Antonio Business Journal, <u>Coaching for a living: New trend in consulting hits San Antonio</u> By Sanford Nowlin, Feb. 23, 1996* ✧
- *San Antonio Business Journal, <u>S.A. professionals get certified for corporate coaching program</u> by Melissa Monroe, Jan. 9-15, 1998* ♣
- *San Antonio Express-News, <u>A recipe for success: Personal coaches provide clients the key ingredients to bolster careers</u> by John Shinal, March 23, 1997* ♣
- *San Bernardino Sun, <u>Hate your job? Feel like you're at a dead end? Don't know where to turn? Maybe you need a career coach</u> by Janet Zimmerman, Dec. 28, 1997*
- *San Diego Business Journal, <u>Former wine importer turns to coaching to keep his spirits alive</u> by Mike Allen, Feb. 26, 1996* ✧
- *San Diego Union-Tribune, <u>Personal coaches join fight against life's gremlins</u> by Kay Harvey, May 4, 1998* ♣
- *San Diego Union-Tribune, <u>Tips from the sidelines: career coaches have growing role in ever-changing marketplace</u> by Michael Kinsman, Oct. 21, 1996* ♣
- *San Francisco Chronicle, <u>Career coaches help you climb to the top</u>, by Ilana DeBare. May 4, 1998* ♣
- *San Jose Mercury News, <u>Do You Need an Executive Coach</u>? by Sherri Eng, March 13, 1996* ✧
- *San Jose Mercury News, **ADD TITLE**, by Michelle Quinn, May, 1998* ✧
- *Santa Cruz Sentinel, <u>Personal best: "Life" coaches provide private, professional motivation</u> by Jennifer Pittman, Jan. 18, 1998* ♣
- *Seattle Post-Intelligencer, <u>Corporate Coaches May Help You Get Ahead</u> by Carol Smith, March 1996* ✧ ♣
- *Seattle Times, March 1996*

I-6

- *Self Magazine, Dec. 1996*
- *Sharing Ideas Magazine, by Mary Gardner Marcoccia, May 1998*
- *SHE Magazine (New Zealand) by Joanna Wayne, 1998*
- *South China Morning Post Magazine, <u>Getting a Life</u> by Tessa Souter, April 13, 1997*
- *South Florida Business Journal, <u>Calling in a coach</u>: <u>The growing trend is to hire a personal trainer for your career</u> by Hortense Leon, March 7, 1997 ✤*
- *Southwest Airlines Magazine, Feb. 1996*
- *State Journal-Register (Springfield, IL), <u>Hey coach, I need your help: More owners get aid to make business click</u> by Natalie Boehme, May 20, 1997 ✤*
- *Strategic Edge (Economics Press), <u>Can "personal coaches" boost careers and company performance</u>? March 1997 ✤*
- *Tampa Tribune Times, <u>A New Kind of Helper</u> by Kathleen Driscoll, April 1996 ✧*
- *Tampa Tribune Times, <u>Send me in, Coach</u>! by Tom Jackson, April 28, 1996 ✧*
- *Tampa Tribune, <u>Are You a Candidate for a Personal Coach</u>? ✧*
- *Techweb.com (CMP Publications), by Dave Johnson, 1998*
- *Telegraph (Nashua, NH), Aug., 1996*
- *Ticker, <u>Coach time</u> by Jackie Day, Oct./Nov. 1996 ✤*
- *Trailer Life Magazine, Sept. 1996*
- *Training, <u>Hey, coach...Sports coaches still prowl the sidelines of the motivational speaking business, but is anyone listening to them</u>? by David Stamps, December, 1996 ✤*
- *Tribune Media Services' College Press Service*
- *Tribune Newspapers, <u>Personal coach can help you succeed in game of life</u> by Carrie White, Feb. 24, 1996*
- *Tuscon Citizen, <u>Coaches Help Rally Careers</u> by Jennifer Cushman, March 1996 ✧*
- *TWA Ambassador, Nov.r 1996*
- *U.S. News & World Report, Oct. 28, 1996 ✤*
- *USA Today, <u>University Trains Coaches for the Game of Life</u> by Craig Wilson, May 1996 ✧*
- *Vancouver (BC) Province, <u>Coach's Lofty Mission: Clients taught how to live a better life</u> by Paul Luke, Feb. 27, 1996 ✧*
- *Ve'adim (Israeli business magazine), by Daniella Ashkenazy, Summer, 1997 ✤ (in Hebrew)*
- *Wall Street Journal*
- *Wall Walla Union Bulletin*
- *Washington Times, 1997*
- *Washington Post, <u>First Come Goals, Then Guts and</u>*

*Glory. In the Growing Field of Executive Coaching, a
Virginia Counselor Advances Women's Ambitions*
by Sandra Evans October 5, 1998 ❖
- Washington Post, *Guidance From the Sidelines: Part
Counselor, Part Mentor, Part Cheerleader, the
"Business Coach" Is a New Addition to Corporate
Rosters* by Amy Joyce, June 28, 1998 ❖
- *Wirtschaftswoche (German business magazine),
Paid Friends* by Brigitte v. Haacke, July 3, 1997 ❖
(English)
- *Women as Managers, Put me in, coach!* July 7, 1997 ♣
- *Workforce Diversity, In your corner: Stuck in a career
rut? why not hire a coach to lend support and direct
your professional growth and development? by
Rosanne Beers, Summer, 1996*
- *Workforce Diversity, Winter 1996*

PUBLICATIONS ON COACHING:

- Professional Coach - Published since 1996 by the
Professional Coaches and Mentors Association for
members and subscribers. Contact: Susan Harrison,
PCMA, 10681 Chestnut, Los Alamitos, CA 90720.
Tel: 562-799-2421, Fax: 562-799-2423.
E-mail: ProCoach@Pacbell.net.

- Priorities, The Journal of Personal and Professional
Success - Published by Franklin Covey Co.,
2200 West Parkway Blvd., Salt Lake City, UT 84119.
E-mail: priorities@franklincovey.com
Web: www.franklincovey.com

COACHES THAT WRITE REGULAR COLUMNS ON COACHING OR HAVE REGULAR TV OR RADIO SHOWS ON COACHING TOPICS:

- Crain's Detroit Business, "Coaching" by Bill Pinkerton
- Midrange Management Review, "Coach's Corner"
by Bill Pinkerton
- New York Post, career columnist, Judy Rosemarin
- Raleigh (NC) Sunday News & Observer, "Dear Career
Coach" by Temple Porter
- San Luis Obispo County Telegram-Tribune, "Business
Success" by Don Maruska
- Syndicated, "Practical Psychology" by Lloyd Thomas
- Telecom Reseller, "Coach's Corner" by Bill Pinkerton

COACH U CHAPTERS WORLDWIDE

North America
Canada
Alberta
British Columbia
Nova Scotia
Ontario
Quebec
United States
Alaska
Arizona
California
Colorado
Connecticut
Florida
Georgia
Hawaii
Idaho
Illinois
Iowa
Louisiana
Maryland
Massachusetts
Michigan
Minnesota
Missouri
Montana
Nebraska
Nevada
New Hampshire
New Jersey
New Mexico
New York
North Carolina
Ohio
Oregon
Pennsylvania
Rhode Island
Tennessee
Texas
Utah
Vermont
Virginia
Washington
Wisconsin

Europe & Russia
Austria
Belgium
Cypress

Germany
Italy
Norway
Sweden
UK

Africa
Angola

Middle East
Israel

Central & South America, Carribean
Virgin Islands

Australia, India, Pacific Islands
Australia
Hong Kong
Japan
New Zealand
Singapore

We are adding chapters all the time. Contact worldhost@coachu.com to find out if there is a Coach U chapter near you.

Coaching Goals

Achieve
↓
Solve Problem
↓
Redesign Life
↓
Learn New Skills
↓
Make Change
↓
Create Something

Not passive
Partnership
collab.

Why Coaching Works

Honesty Openness
Collaboration

diagnostic tool: What part
of our relationship
is weakest for you?

coaching ←→ therapy
achievement   not achievement

coaching ←→ consulting
who   how, what